Nacimientos

Nacimientos

Nativity Scenes by Southwest Indian Artisans

Weihnachtskrippen von Indianischen Kunsthandwerkern des Südwestens

Nacimientos Hechos por Artistas Indios del Suroeste

by Guy and Doris Monthan

Avanyu Publishing Inc. / Albuquerque, New Mexico

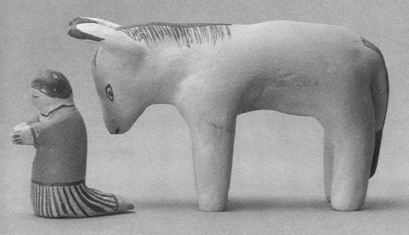

Cover:
Plains Indian Nativity by Manuel Vigil
of Tesuque Pueblo, New Mexico

Weihnachtskrippe der Prairieindianer
von Manuel Vigil, Tesuque Pueblo,
New Mexico

Nacimiento de los Indios de la
Tribu Plains, hecho por Manuel Vigil
del Pueblo Tesuque en Nuevo México

Title Page:
Detail / Einzelheit / Detalle
from Nacimiento by
Helen Cordero (see page 27)

to Veronica and Bill Monthan

First Edition Published by Northland Press, 1979
Designed by Guy Monthan

21874667

CHANGES: 1979 TO 1990

In the little over a decade since *Nacimientos* was first published, significant changes have taken place. The number of Nativity artisans has more than tripled and where Cochiti, Santa Clara, and Tesuque Pueblos were the major producers (in that order), it is now Jemez, Cochiti, and Acoma; prices have escalated, particularly among the better known artisans; a few older artists have dropped out through natural attrition, but a far larger group of younger artists has entered the field. Two new sources have been added to the original fourteen pueblos and tribes: the Yaqui tribe in Southern Arizona and Zuni Pueblo in Western New Mexico, where Claudia Cellición is making Nativities in beadwork.

Of the thirty-seven artists recorded in this book, twenty-eight are still engaged in the craft. Manuel Vigil, the first pueblo Nativity artisan, whose charming creations are copiously illustrated here, died on March 28th of this year, just short of his

VERÄNDERUNGEN: VON 1979 BIS 1990

In den etwas mehr als zehn Jahren seit *Nacimientos* erstmals erschien, haben einige bedeutsame Veränderungen stattgefunden. Die Zahl der Kunsthandwerker, die sich mit der Herstellung von Weihnachtskrippen befaßen, hat sich mehr als verdreifacht, und wo Cochiti, Santa Clara und Tesuque Pueblos die Hauptproduzenten waren (und zwar in genau dieser Reihenfolge), sind es nun Jemez, Cochiti und Acoma. Die Preise sind, vor allem unter den besser bekannten Kunsthandwerkern, sprunghaft angestiegen. Infolge altersbedingter natürlicher Selektion sind einige der älteren Künstler ausgeschieden. Dafür hat aber eine bei weitem größere Gruppe von jüngeren Künstlern dieses Kunsthandwerk ergriffen. Zwei neue Quellen wurden den ursprünglich vierzehn Pueblos und Stämmen hinzugefügt: der Stamm der Yaquis im südlichen Arizona und das Zuni Pueblo im Westen von New Mexico, wo Claudia Cellición Weihnachtskrippen aus Perlen herstellt.

Von den in diesem Buch aufgeführten siebenunddreißig Künstlern sind noch achtundzwanzig in diesem Kunsthandwerk tätig. Der erste Pueblo-Krippenbauer, Manuel Vigil, dessen entzückende Werke hier zahlreich abgebildet sind, starb am 28.

CAMBIOS: DE 1979 A 1990

En los once años que han transcurrido desde que *Nacimientos* vió la luz del día, han ocurrido cambios importantes. El número de artesanos dedicados a hacer Nacimientos se ha triplicado. Por su parte, los indios de los pueblos Cochiti, Santa Clara y Tesuque (en este orden) quienes in el pasado fueron los más productivos, han sido, hoy día, ultrapasados por los de Jemez, Cochiti y Acoma; los precios han subido enormemente, en particular los de los artesanos más conocidos; algunos de los más viejos han desaparecido debido a causas naturales, pero un numeroso grupo de artesanos jóvenes ha tomado su lugar. Dos nuevos grupos se han sumado a los catorce pueblos y tribus iniciales: la tribu de los Yaqui, en el sur de Arizona, y el pueblo Zuni, en el oeste de New Mexico, donde Claudia Cellición hace Nacimientos con abalorios.

De los treinta y siete artistas mencionados in este libro, veintiocho todavía continúan dedicándose a este tipo de artesanía. Manuel Vigil, el pionero de los artistas dedicados a hacer Nacimientos, y cuyas obras están copiosamente representadas in este libro, murió el 28 de marzo de

ninetieth birthday. Vicenta, his wife and co-creator of Nativities, is no longer active, but three of their children are: Jennie Valdez and Arthur Vigil of Tesuque and Anna Marie Lovato of Santo Domingo. Two other artists have died—Chepa Franco of the Papago tribe and, in Santa Clara, Luther Gutierrez of the "Margaret and Luther" team. However, Margaret continues in their distinctive style. At Cochiti Pueblo, Frances Suina and Felipa Trujillo, both now in their eighties, no longer work. Helen Cordero still makes her famous Storyteller dolls and Nativities assisted by her daughter, Tony Suina, and grandchildren.

Most of the artists listed at the back of the book are currently active. Stella Teller, who has initiated a revival of pottery art in her native Isleta, has brought four of her daughters into the field. Mary Toya of Jemez is prolific in both her artistic and maternal production; she has seven daughters now making Nativities. It is interesting to note that Mary and her five sisters, all Nativity artists, have twenty-nine children between them, over half of whom make Nativities as well. Many of the second generation Nativity artists are already instructing their own young children in the art, thus insuring a tradition that will extend long into the future.

März dieses Jahres, kurz vor seinem neunzigsten Geburtstag. Seine Frau und Mitarbeiterin an den Weihnachtskrippen, Vicenta, ist nicht mehr in diesem Kunsthandwerk tätig, dafür aber drei ihrer Kinder: Jeannie Valdez und Arthur Vigil aus Tesuque und Anna Marie Lovato aus Santo Domingo. Zwei weitere Künstler sind zwischenzeitlich verstorben—Chepa Franco vom Stamm der Papagos und Luther Gutierrez, einer der beiden Partner im Künstlerteam "Margaret und Luther," in Santa Clara. Margaret jedoch führt ihre Arbeit in ihrem unverwechselbaren Stil fort. In Cochiti Pueblo sind Frances Suina und Felipa Trujillo nicht mehr als Krippenbauer tätig. Beide sind mittlerweile schon über 80 Jahre alt. Helen Cordero fertigt immer noch ihre berühmten Puppen, die Geschichtenerzähler, und Krippen an. Ihre Tochter, Tony Suina, und ihre Enkelkinder sind ihr dabei behilflich.

Die meisten der am Ende des Buches aufgeführten Künstler sind gegenwärtig in diesem Kunsthandwerk tätig. Stella Teller, die eine Wiederbelebung der Töpferkunst in ihrem Heimatort Isleta eingeleitet hat, führte vier ihrer Töchter in diese Kunst ein. Maria Toya aus Jemez ist sowohl in ihrer Tätigkeit als Künstlerin wie auch als Mutter sehr produktiv. Sie hat insgesamt sieben Töchter, die jetzt Weihnachtskrippen herstellen. Interessant ist, daß Mary und ihre fünf Schwestern, die sich alle mit der Herstellung von Weihnachtskrippen befassen, insgesamt neunundzwanzig Kinder haben, von denen über die Hälfte auch Krippenbauer sind.

Viele der Künstler, die in der zweiten Generation Weihnachtskrippen bauen, unterrichten nun schon ihre eigenen Kinder in diesem Kunsthandwerk und sichern so den Fortbestand einer Tradition, die sich noch weit in die Zukunft erstrecken wird.

este año, faltándole uno para cumplir su nonagésimo aniversario. Vicenta, su esposa y coautor de Nacimientos, está en el retiro, pero tres de sus hijos: Jennie Valdez y Arthur Vigil de Tesuque, así como Anna Marie Lovato de Santo Domingo continúan haciéndolos. Otros dos artistas que han fallecido son: Chepa Franco, de la tribu Papago, y Luther Gutiérrez, de la pareja "Margaret y Luther" de Santa Clara. Margaret, sin embargo, sigue adelante manteniendo el mismo estilo con el que eran conocidos. En el pueblo de Cochiti, Frances Suina y Felipa Trujillo, ambos de más de ochenta años, ya no trabajan. Helen Cordero sigue haciendo sus famosos Nacimientos y su conocida figura el Narrador de Cuentos (Storyteller), ayudada en ello por sus nietos y por Tony Suina, su hija.

La mayoría de los artistas enumerados al final del libro siguen en activo. Stella Teller, quien ha iniciado un renacimiento de la alfarería en Isleta, donde ella nació, ha incorporado a cuatro de sus hijas a dicha actividad. Mary Toya, de Jemez, es fecunda tanto como madre y como artista; sus siete hijas siguen sus pasos. Es interesante el saber que Mary y sus cinco hermanas, todas ellas artistas dedicadas a hacer Nacimientos, tienen un total de veintinueve descendientes, la mitad de los cuales, asimismo, hacen Nacimientos. Muchos de los artistas pertenecientes a la segunda generación, están educando a sus descendientes en este arte, lo que garantiza que dicha tradición se mantendrá por largo tiempo.

CONTENTS INHALT CONTENIDO

"Let us go to Bethlehem and see this thing that has
  happened which the Lord has made known to us."   Luke 2:15

"Laβt uns gehen nach Bethlehem und die Geschichte sehen, die
  da geschehen ist, die uns der Herr kundgetan hat."   Lukas 2:15

"Vamos a Belén a ver esta cosa que ha ocurrido, lo cual Dios nos ha
  hecho conocido."   Lucas 2:15

PREFACE   VORWORT   PRÓLOGO

This book began as an idea for an article four years ago. In the fall of 1975, the Museum of Northern Arizona in Flagstaff presented a month-long Christmas exhibit, *Nacimientos: Manger Scenes from the Sallie R. Wagner Collection.* Featured were Nativities by a dozen or more New Mexican artisans — several carved-wood scenes by Hispanic-American artists and at least seven by Pueblo Indian potters. Among the latter was one artist we knew, Helen Cordero of Cochiti Pueblo. In 1972 we photographed one of her Nativities to be included along with her other ceramic figures in our book, *Art and Indian Individualists.* At the time we had assumed she was the only Indian artist doing them. It came as a surprise to discover that there were other Nativity artists in Cochiti as well as in Tesuque and Santa Clara. I suggested to my husband that this small group of Pueblo Nativity artisans could

Vor vier Jahren kamen wir auf den Gedanken, einen Artikel zu schreiben; daraus enstand schließlich dieses Buch. Im Herbst 1975 veranstaltete das Museum von Northern Arizona in Flagstaff eine vierwöchige Weihnachtsausstellung "Nacimientos: Weihnachtskrippen aus der Sallie R. Wagner-Sammlung". Gezeigt wurden Weihnachtskrippen von über einem Dutzend Kunsthandwerkern aus New Mexico — mehrere geschnitzte Szenen von hispano-amerikanischen Künstlern und mindestens sieben von Pueblo Töpferinnen. Unter den letzteren war eine Künstlerin, Helen Cordero aus Cochiti Pueblo, die wir schon kannten. Im Jahre 1972 hatten wir eine ihrer Weihnachtskrippen fotographiert, um diese neben ihren anderen keramischen Figuren in unserem Buch *Kunst und indianische Individualisten* abzubilden. Damals hatten wir angenommen, sie sei die einzige indianische Künstlerin, die Weihnachtskrippen anfertige. Eine Überraschung war es, als wir entdeckten, daß auch andere Künstler sowohl in Cochiti als auch in Tesuque und Santa Clara solche herstellen. Ich schlug meinem Mann vor, diese kleine Gruppe von Pueblo-Kunsthandwerkern in einem

Este libro comenzó hace cuatro años con la idea de publicar un artículo. En el otoño de 1975, el Museo del Norte de Arizona en Flagstaff presentó por un mes una exposición de Navidad, *Nacimientos: Escenas de pesebres de la colección de Sallie R. Wagner.* Se exhibieron Nacimientos de una docena ó más de artesanos de Nuevo México, varias escenas de madera tallada de artistas hispanoamericanos, y por lo menos siete de ceramistas de los Indios Pueblo. Entre estos últimos había una artista que nosotros conocíamos, Helen Cordero, del pueblo Cochiti. En 1972 sacamos fotografías de uno de sus Nacimientos para incluirlo junto con sus otras figuras de cerámica en nuestro libro *Arte e individualistas indios.* En ese tiempo supusimos que ella era la única artista india que las hacía. Nos sorprendió descubrir que había otros artistas de Nacimientos en Cochiti así como también en Tesuque y en Santa Clara. Le sugerí a mi esposo que este pequeño grupo de artesanos pueblos de Nacimientos podría ser el

Detail / Einzelheit / Detalle from Nacimiento by Alfred Aguilar (see page 62)

be the subject of an interesting little article, and a few days after Christmas we set out for New Mexico. Little did we know then what an odyssey we were embarking upon!

On that first trip and subsequent trips during 1976, our list of artists multiplied, and we had more than enough photographs to illustrate our "little article" but very little in the way of a text. Extensive searches in libraries produced no answers to these questions: When had the making of Nativities first surfaced as an art form among southwest Indian artisans? Had Christian symbolism appeared in any of their other art forms, and when? Interviews with museum personnel, Indian art dealers, and collectors produced tantalizing bits and pieces but no really solid background material. The disparity between the increasing number of artists who had turned to the Nativity theme and the lack of any literature on the subject was intriguing. "You know," I said to my husband, "this deserves to be a book." The first proposal we submitted to Northland Press included Hispanic-American artists, but in the following year we discovered so many more Indian artisans that we decided to confine the book to them.

Our odyssey had taken us on more than twenty field trips throughout New Mexico and Arizona and countless

interessanten kurzen Artikel zu behandeln, und wenige Tage nach Weihnachten reisten wir nach New Mexico, ohne zu wissen, was für eine Odyssee uns bevorstand.

Während jener ersten Reise und darauffolgenden Reisen im Jahre 1976 verlängerte sich unsere Liste von Künstlern, und wir hatten mehr als genug Bilder, um unseren "kurzen Artikel" zu illustrieren, aber sehr wenig Material, das als Text dienen konnte. Ausgedehnte Nachforschungen in Bibliotheken brachten keine Antworten auf die Fragen: Wann war die Herstellung von Weihnachtskrippen als Kunstform zum ersten Mal unter den südwestindianischen Kunsthandwerkern aufgetaucht? Waren christliche Symbole in ihren anderen Kunstformen erschienen? Wenn ja, wann? Interviews mit Museumspersonal, Indianerkunsthändlern und Sammlern brachten verlockende Bruckstücke von Informationen hervor, aber nichts, was als solides Hintergrundmaterial dienen konnte. Die Tatsache, daß trotz der wachsenden Zahl von Weihnachtskrippenmachern bisher nichts über diese Kunstform geschrieben worden war, erregte unser Interesse. "Weißt du", sagte ich zu meinem Mann, "dieses Thema sollte eigentlich in einem Buch behandelt werden." Der erste Vorschlag, den wir dem Northland-Verlag unterbreiteten, schloß auch hispano-amerikanische Künstler ein, aber im folgenden Jahr entdeckten wir so viele neue indianische Künstler, daß wir uns entschlossen, das Buch auf sie zu beschränken.

Unsere odyssee hatte zu mehr als zwanzig Exkursionen durch New Mexico und Arizona geführt und zu zahllosen

tema de un interesante y pequeño artículo, y pocos días después de Navidad partimos para Nuevo México. ¡No nos imaginábamos que nos estábamos embarcando en una gran odisea!

En aquella primera visita y las subsiguientes durante 1976, nuestra lista de artistas se multiplicó, y tuvimos suficientes fotografías para ilustrar nuestro "pequeño artículo," pero teníamos muy poco para el texto. Investigaciones extensivas en las bibliotecas no produjeron respuestas a las siguientes preguntas: ¿Cuándo había aparecido la creación de Nacimientos como un arte entre los artesanos indios del Suroeste? ¿Había surgido el simbolismo cristiano en alguna de las otras formas artísticas, y cuándo? Entrevistas con personal de museos, con vendedores de arte indio, y con coleccionistas aportaron trozos tentadores de información pero no realmente un material de fondo sólido. Es curiosa la falta de información sobre el tema de los Nacimientos frente a un aumento del número de artistas que se dedican a ese tema. "Sabes," le dije a mi esposo, "esto merece ser un libro." La primera propuesta que presentamos a Northland Press incluía artistas hispanoamericanos, pero al año siguiente descubrimos tantos otros artesanos indios que decidimos limitarnos a éstos.

Nuestra odisea había durado más de veinte incursiones a través de Nuevo

photographing sessions and interviews. All of the seventeen artists whose work is illustrated in this book were interviewed personally and, with two exceptions, in their own homes, where we often saw their Nativities in various stages of production. A list of twenty additional artists is given at the end of the book, bringing the total known to us to thirty-seven, representing fourteen pueblos and tribes. This should be amended to "known to us at this time," since each week seems to bring another artist to our attention. Many of these have done Nativities in the past; others are just entering the field.

Several decisions were made that should be clarified. The Spanish term for Nativities, *Nacimientos,* was chosen for the title because it is the term most often used in New Mexico, where most of the Nativities featured here originated. Another decision was to photograph most of the scenes without the manger settings. Though these enhance the scenes when displayed where they may be viewed from different angles, they distract attention from the figures themselves when presented in the two-dimensional restrictions of the printed page. For a similar reason, miniature sets are not illustrated. Though they are very popular and have great charm when viewed in the perspective of their surroundings, they have of necessity little

fotographischen Sessionen und Inter-views. Jeden der siebzehn Künstler, deren Werke in diesem Buch gezeigt werden, befragten wir persönlich; mit zwei Ausnahmen geschah dies bei ihnen daheim, wo wir ihre Weihnachts-krippen oft in verschiedenen Stadien der Produktion sahen. Eine Liste von zwanzig weiteren Künstlern wird am Ende des Buches angeführt; somit sind es im ganzen siebenunddreißig uns bekannte Künstler, die vierzehn Pueblos und Stämme vertreten; eigentlich sollten wir sagen, "uns bis jetzt bekannte Künstler", denn jede Woche scheint uns einen neuen Namen zur Kenntnis zu bringen. Viele von diesen haben schon früher Weihnachts-krippen angefertigt; andere fangen erst gerade an.

Einige technische Entscheidungen sollen hier erläutert werden. Das spanische Wort für Weihnachtskrippen, *Nacimientos,* haben wir als Titel gewählt, weil man es in New Mexico, dem Staate, wo die meisten der hier abgebildeten Weihnachtskrippen herstammen, am häufigsten gebraucht. Eine weitere Entscheidung betrifft die Abbildungen: die meisten Szenen wurden *ohne* die Weihnachtskrippen fotographiert. Obwohl diese eine aus verschiedenen Blickwinkeln beobachtete Szene bereichern, lenken sie den Blick des Zuschauers von den Gestalten ab, wenn sie im beschränkten zweidimen-sionalen Format der Druckseite gezeigt werden. Aus einem ähnlichen Grunde werden Miniaturgruppen nicht abge-bildet; obwohl sie sehr beliebt sind und aus der Perspektive ihrer Umgebung besonderen Reiz besitzen, mangeln sie notwendigerweise wegen ihrer

México y Arizona y un sin fin de foto-grafías y entrevistas. Todos los diez y siete artistas cuyas obras se ilustran en el libro fueron entrevistados personalmente y, con dos excepciones, en sus propios hogares donde a menudo vimos sus Nacimientos en diferentes etapas de producción. Una lista de veinte artistas más se presenta al fin del libro con un total de treinta y siete que representan catorce pueblos y tribus. Debemos cor-regirnos y decir que "son los que noso-tros conocemos hasta la fecha," ya que cada semana se nos informa de otro artista. Muchos de éstos han creado Nacimientos antes; otros acaban de entrar en este campo.

Tomamos varias decisiones que debe-mos aclarar. Escogimos el vocablo español *Nacimientos* para el título, por-que es el término que más se usa en Nuevo México donde se originó la mayor parte de los Nacimientos. Otra decisión fue sacar fotografías de las escenas sin los escenarios. Aunque éstos embellecen las escenas cuando se exhiben de tal forma que se pueden ver desde ángulos diferentes, distraen la atención de las figuras mismas cuando se presentan en las dos dimensiones restringidas de que la página impresa. Por una razón similar, los juegos en miniatura no aparecen ilustrados. Aunque son muy populares y poseen un encanto especial, cuando se los ve desde la perspectiva de su ambi-ente, tienen, por necesidad, pocos

detailing and do not show up to best advantage in photographs. The decision to print the book in German and Spanish as well as English was prompted by the fact that the Nativity tradition is very strong in Europe and Latin America.

We received help and encouragement from many people, first among them, Sallie R. Wagner of Santa Fe. At the Museum of New Mexico and the Museum of International Folk Art, we received consistent aid from George Ewing, Dr. Yvonne Lange, Kristin Eppler, Elizabeth Buchanan, and Charlene Cerny. We are also grateful to Dorothy Vaughter of the Museum of Northern Arizona, Flagstaff; Marilyn Vatter of Denver; Alexander E. Anthony, Jr., and Katherine H. Rust of Albuquerque; and Anita Thomas of Santa Fe. Father Lambert Fremdling of the Papago reservation helped in more ways than we can enumerate. Three major collectors to whom we are indebted are Dr. Maria Elisabeth Houtzager, Utrecht, Netherlands; Rosemary D. Sullivan, Brooklyn, New York; and Dr. and Mrs. Zigmund Kosicki, Santa Fe. Our special thanks for many graces go to Gene Meany Hodge of Santa Fe.

DORIS MONTHAN

Kleinheit an Details, und zeigen sich in Fotographien nicht aufs vorteilhafteste. Der Entschluß, das Buch sowohl auf Englisch als auch auf Deutsch und Spanisch zu veröffentlichen, beruht auf der Tatsache, daß die Weihnachts-krippentradition in Europa und Latein-amerika sehr stark ausgeprägt ist.

Viele Leute — vor allem Sallie R. Wagner aus Santa Fe — haben uns Hilfe und Unterstützung gewährt. Im Museum von New Mexico und im Museum für Internationale Volkskunst haben uns George Ewing, Dr. Yvonne Lange, Kristin Eppler, Elizabeth Buchanan und Charlene Cerny stets hilfsbereit zur Seite gestanden. Wir sind auch Dorothy Vaughter des Museums von Northern Arizona in Flagstaff, Marilyn Vatter aus Denver, Alexander E. Anthony, Jr. und Katherine H. Rust aus Albuquerque, und Anita Thomas aus Santa Fe, sehr dankbar. Father Lambert Fremdling vom Papago-Reservat hat uns auf vielerlei Weise — mehr als wir hier im einzelnen aufzählen können — geholfen. Drei führenden Sammlern — Dr. Maria Elizabeth Houtzager aus Utrecht, Rosemary D. Sullivan aus Brooklyn, New York, Dr. Zigmund Kosicki und seiner Frau aus Santa Fe, New Mexico — sind wir zu Dank verpflichtet. Für all ihr Wohlwollen gebührt an dieser Stelle unser besonderer Dank Gene Meany Hodge aus Santa Fe.

DORIS MONTHAN

detalles, y sus mejores cualidades no aparecen en fotografías. La decisión de imprimir el libro en alemán y español, así como también en inglés, se originó en el hecho de que la tradición de Naci-mientos es muy fuerte en Europa y America Latina.

Hemos recibido ayudo y estímulo de muchas personas, entre ellas, la primera, Sallie R. Wagner de Santa Fe en el Museo de Nuevo México y el Museo de Arte Folklórico Internacional. Recibimos ayuda constante de George Ewing, Dr. Yvonne Lange, Kristin Eppler, Elizabeth Buchanan, y Charlene Cerny. Estamos agradecidos a Dorothy Vaughter del Museo del Norte de Arizona, Flagstaff; a Marilyn Vatter de Denver; a Alexander E. Anthony, Jr., y Katherine H. Rust de Albuquerque; y a Anita Thomas de Santa Fe. El Padre Lambert Fremdling de la Reservación Pápago, nos ayudó en más formas de las que podemos enumerar. Tres coleccionistas a quienes les estamos sumamente agradecidos son: la Dra. María Elisabeth Houtzager, Utrecht, Países Bajos; Rosemary D. Sullivan, Brooklyn, New York; y el Dr. y la Sra. Zigmund Kosicki, Santa Fe. Nuestro agradecimiento muy especial a Gene Meany Hodge de Santa Fe por sus muchas atenciones.

DORIS MONTHAN

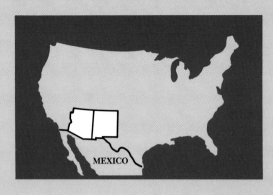

MAP OF INDIAN PUEBLOS

KARTE DER INDIANER-PUEBLOS

MAPA DE LOS PUEBLOS INDIOS

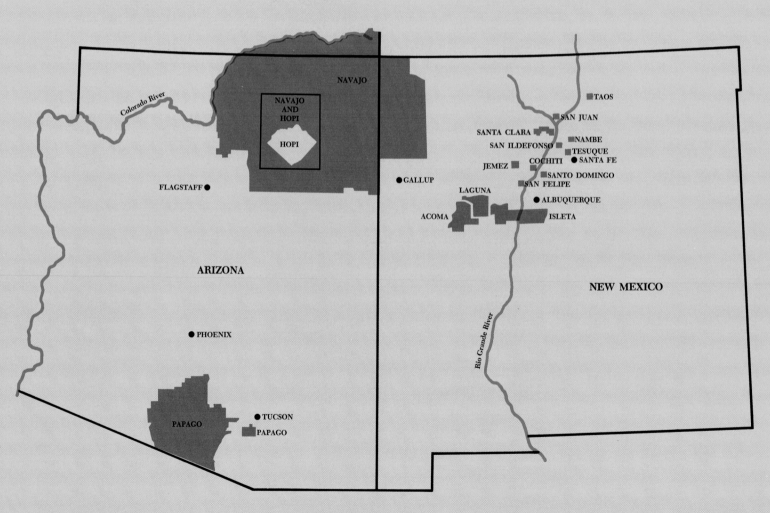

INTRODUCTION   EINLEITUNG   INTRODUCCIÓN

A new phenomenon has emerged among the Indian artisans of the southwestern United States — the making of Nativity scenes. This universally popular art form has flourished in Europe since the sixteenth century and is known in every language for its focal point, the crib of the Infant Christ — *Crèche* in France, *Krippe* in Germany, *Presepio* in Italy, *Belem* in Portugal, and *Pesebre* in Spain, to name a few. In the Spanish-speaking countries of the Western Hemisphere and in Puerto Rico and New Mexico, the name for the crib and attendant figures is *Nacimiento*.

According to the earliest collectors, the first Indian-made Nativities appeared in the late 1950s. Into the early 1960s, the craft was engaged in by only three or four artisans on an occasional basis. It accelerated in the late 1960s and swelled to the proportions of a movement in the late 1970s. Two of the most intriguing aspects of this phenomenon

Eine Neuerung ist unter den indianischen Künstlern des amerikanischen Südwestens in Erscheinung getreten — die Darstellung von Krippenszenen. Diese universell volkstümliche Kunstform blüht in Europa seit dem sechzehnten Jahrhundert, und sie wird in jeder Sprache nach dem Mittelpunkt der Darstellung benannt, der Krippe des Jesuskindes: *Creche* in Frankreich, Krippe in Deutschland, *Presepio* in Italien, *Belem* in Portugal und *Pesebre* in Spanien, um nur einige zu nennen. In den spanisch sprechenden Ländern der westlichen Hemisphäre, ebenso in Puerto Rico und New Mexico, wird der Ausdruck *Nacimiento* für die Krippe und die sie umgebenden Figuren verwendet.

Die frühesten Sammler berichten, daß die ersten indianischen Krippendarstellungen in den späten 1950er Jahren auftauchten. Bis in die frühen sechziger Jahre übten nur drei oder vier Künstler gelegentlich dieses Kunstgewerbe aus. Während der späten sechziger Jahre nahm die Herstellung von Krippen rasch zu und erreichte in den späten 1970er Jahren das Ausmaß einer echten künstlerischen Bewegung. Zwei der faszinierendsten Aspekte dieser

Un fenómeno nuevo ha surgido entre los artesanos indios del suroeste de los Estados Unidos — la creación de escenas de Nacimientos. Esta forma de arte, universalmente popular, florecía en Europa desde el siglo XVI y es conocido en todos los idiomas por su tema principal: la cuna del Niño Jesús — *Creche* en Francia, *Krippe* en Alemania, *Presepio* en Italia, *Belem* en Portugal, y *Pesebre* en España, para nombrar unos pocos. En los países que habla español del Hemisferio Occidental, así como en Puerto Rico y Nuevo México, el nombre de la cuna y las figuras que la acompañan es *Nacimiento*.

Según los primeros coleccionistas, los primeros Nacimientos hechos por indios aparecieron en los últimos años de la década de 1950. A principios de la década de 1960, sólo tres o cuatro artistas se dedicaban a este arte ocasionalmente. Este ritmo se aceleró en los últimos años de la década de 1960 y adquirió las proporciones de un verdadero movimiento en los últimos años de la década de 1970. Dos de los aspectos más intrigantes de este fenómeno son

are that it has gone unrecorded and that it is the first widespread expression of the Christian religion to emerge among the many art forms of the southwest Indian. A few Indian painters have occasionally dealt with Christian themes, silversmiths have made many crosses for necklaces or even an altarpiece on commission, but no single theme done on a consistent basis by a large number of artists — that might qualify as a movement — has been noted prior to the emergence of the Nativity scene.

Crib devotion began in early Christian years at the birthplace of Christ in Bethlehem. The tradition was almost extinguished by the emperor Hadrian but revived again in A.D. 326 by Constantine the Great and his mother Saint Helena.[1] From there it spread to other parts of the world. There are fourth century carvings in the catacombs of Rome that depict the Holy Family, the Three Kings, shepherds, ox, ass, and sheep. Frescos of the Nativity scene dating to the seventh or eighth century were found on the walls of a church in Egypt. The first known freestanding figures were created in the thirteenth century by Arnolfo de Cambio and may still be seen at the Basilica of the Santa Maria Maggiore in Rome.[2] In the fifteenth and sixteenth centuries, Italian artists created large

Erscheinung sind die Tatsachen, daß diese Bewegung bisher nicht dokumentiert wurde, und daß sie der erste weitverbreitete Ausdruck christlicher Religion ist, der aus den vielgestaltigen Kunstformen der südwestlichen Indianer hervortritt. Einige wenige indianische Maler haben sich gelegentlich mit christlichen Motiven befaßt, Silberschmiede haben zahlreiche Kreuze für Halsketten oder, auf Bestellung, sogar als Altarschmuck hergestellt. Jedoch fand sich bis zum Auftreten der Krippendarstellung kein anderes Motiv, mit dem sich eine große Anzahl von Künstlern auf längere Zeit befaßt hätte, oder das zu einer echten künstlerischen Bewegung geführt hätte.

Die Anbetung der Krippe begann in den frühchristlichen Jahren, am Geburtsort Christi, in Bethlehem. Diese Tradition wurde unter der Regierung Kaiser Hadrians beinahe ausgelöscht, aber im Jahre 326 durch Konstantin und seine Mutter St. Helena wieder neu belebt.[1] Von dort verbreitete sich die Tradition über andere Länder. In den römischen Katakomben gibt es Skulpturen, auf denen die Heilige Familie, die drei Könige, Schäfer, Ochs, Esel und Schafe dargestellt sind. Fresken der Krippenszene, aus dem siebten oder achten Jahrhundert stammend, wurden auf den Wänden einer Kirche in Ägypten gefunden. Die ersten bekannten freistehenden Figuren wurden im dreizehnten Jahrhundert von Arnolfo de Cambio geschaffen, und sie können heute noch in der Basilika Santa Maria Maggiore in Rom gesehen werden.[2] Während des fünfzehnten und sechzehnten Jahrhunderts schufen italienische Künstler große Krippenfiguren von

que esta expresión de arte no ha sido registrada y que es la primera expresión generalizada de la religión Cristiana que emerge entre las variadas formas de arte del indio del Suroeste. Ocasionalmente, algunos pintores indios han tratado con temas Cristianos; los plateros han hecho innumerables cruces para collares e inclusive, por encargo especial, decoraciones para altares, pero ningún tema especial hecho en forma constante por un grupo numeroso de artistas — que muchos califican como un movimiento — se había notado antes de la emergencia de las creaciones de las escenas de Nacimientos.

La veneración de la cuna empezó en los primeros años del Cristianismo en el mismo lugar del nacimiento de Jesucristo, Belén. Esta tradición casi fue extinguida por el emperador Adrián, pero se revivió nuevamente en el año 326 por Constantino el Grande y su madre Santa Elena.[1] De allí se extendió a otras partes del mundo. En las catacumbas de Roma hay labrados que datan del siglo IV en los que están representados la Sagrada Familia, los Tres Reyes, pastores, bueyes, burros, y ovejas. En las paredes de una iglesia en Egipto se encontraron frescos que datan del siglo VII o del siglo VIII. Las primeras figuras de bulto que se conocieron fueron creadas por Arnolfo de Cambio en el siglo XIII y todavía se pueden admirar en la Basílica de Santa Maria Maggiore en Roma.[2] En los siglos XV y XVI, los artistas italianos crearon grandes figuras

Nativity figures of increasing realism. The earliest scenes with smaller figures were created in Bavaria and the Tyrol, and this approach spread rapidly to Italy, Spain, and France. It is believed that the first Nativity for home use was made in the 1560s for the Duchess of Amalfi.[3]

In addition to the Holy Family, most European Nativities include the Three Wise Men, the shepherds, and animals, but often they include more figures — in some sets, the citizens of an entire village, from the butcher to the candlestick maker. Sets may be elaborate, such as the one created for the King of Naples in 1760, which contains 500 figures costumed in silks and brocades cut from the queen's gowns,[4] or simple and rustic, done in more modest materials. Figures have been made of everything — from wood, clay, tin, or wax, to ivory and precious metals, or, as in one area of Germany, from dried fruits and nuts.[5] Settings vary from just a manger to grandiose re-creations of a palace or village complete with backdrops of mountains, streams, and trees. Some of the most famous artists of each period have turned their talents to the making of Nativities, while at other times Nativities have been made by peasants in their cottages on long winter nights. Each scene reflects the costumes and customs of the artist's own region,

steigendem Realismus. Die ersten Szenen mit kleineren Figuren wurden in Bayern und in Tirol hergestellt, und diese Methode breitete sich rasch nach Italien, Spanien und Frankreich aus. Man vermutet, daß die erste Krippendarstellung für den Hausgebrauch in den 1560er Jahren für die Fürstin von Amalfi gemacht wurde.[3]

Die meisten europäischen Krippen bestehen, neben der Heiligen Familie, aus den heiligen drei Königen, den Schäfern und den Tieren, aber oft werden mehr Figuren hinzugefügt, die Bewohner eines ganzen Dorfes, vom Bürgermeister bis zum Bettler. Der Figurensatz kann so umfangreich sein wie der für den König von Neapel aus dem Jahre 1760, der 500 Figuren enthält, die in Seide und Brokat von den Kleidern der Königin gekleidet sind,[4] oder er kann einfach und ländlich in bescheidene Stoffe gekleidet sein. Man hat die Figuren aus allen erdenklichen Materialien gemacht, aus Holz, Ton, Blech, Wachs, bis zum Elfenbein und Edelmetallen, oder, wie in einer Gegend in Deutschland, aus getrockneten Früchten und Nüssen.[5] Die Szenerie reicht von der einfachen Krippe bis zur grandiosen Nachbildung eines Palastes, oder eines Dorfes vor einem Hintergrund mit Bergen, Flüssen und Bäumen. Einige der berühmtesten Künstler jeder Epoche haben ihr Talent bei der Krippendarstellung bewiesen, während Krippen auf der anderen Seite von bescheidenen Landleuten während langer Winterabende in ihren Hütten gebastelt wurden. Jede Krippenszene aber zeigt die Mode und Bräuche aus der Heimat des betreffenden Künstlers, und sie ermöglicht

de un realismo creciente. Las primeras escenas con figuras más pequeñas fueron hechas en Bavaria y en el Tirol, y este estilo se extendió rápidamente a Italia, España, y Francia. Se cree que el primer Nacimiento para uso doméstico se hizo en 1560 para la Duquesa de Amalfi.[3]

Además de la Sagrada Familia, la mayoría de los Nacimientos europeos incluyen a los Tres Reyes Magos, los pastores, y animales, pero con frecuencia se agregan figuras representativas de una aldea entera, desde el carnicero hasta el fabricante de candeleros. Los juegos pueden ser muy elaborados, como el que se hizo para el Rey de Nápoles en 1760, el cual contenía 500 figuras vestidas en sedas y brocados cortados de los mismos vestidos de la reina,[4] o pueden ser sencillos y rústicos, hechos de materiales más modestos. Se han hecho figuras de materiales muy diversos, como de madera, arcilla, estaño, cera, o también de marfil y metales preciosos, o como en un lugar de Alemania, de frutas secas y nueces.[5] Las escenas pueden variar desde el humilde establo a recreaciones grandiosas de palacios o una aldea completa con montañas, arroyos, y árboles. Algunos de los artistas más famosos de cada época han dedicado sus talentos a la creación de Nacimientos, mientras que en algunas otras épocas los Nacimientos se han hecho por campesinos refugiados en sus chozas protegiéndose de las frías y largas noches de invierno. Cada escena refleja el vestuario y las costumbres de la región de cada

Detail / Einzelheit / Detalle from Nacimiento
by Felipa Trujillo (see page 41)

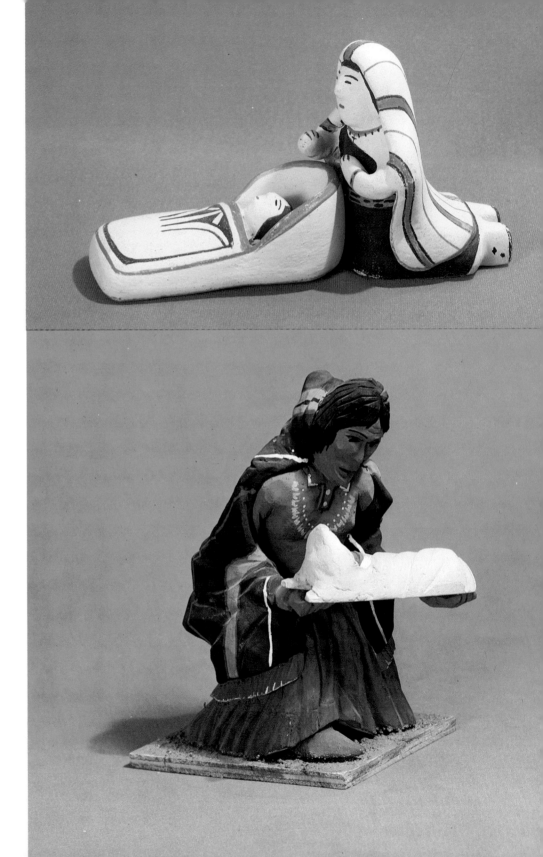

Detail / Einzelheit / Detalle from Nacimiento
by Tom W. Yazzie (see page 53)

4

providing an infinite variety of interpretations. It is a theme that has captivated the interest of people the world over for 2,000 years and shows little sign of diminishing. In Europe today there are hundreds of members of the International Association of Friends of the Crib, with headquarters in Rome and chapters in West Germany, Austria, and France.[6] The tradition is strong in Spain, Mexico, and South America as well.

Oddly enough, at just about the time that the freestanding Nativity figures began flourishing in Europe, the Indians of the Southwest were having their first contact with the European and consequently with the symbols and art forms of the Christian religion. In 1540 when the first expedition of Spanish explorers entered what is now the southwestern United States, the Pueblo Indians already had a religion of their own, as well as highly developed art forms, particularly pottery.[7] The next 300 years of European domination brought a number of changes in the Indians' way of life. Eventually, most accepted the Christian religion, not to supplant their own, but rather as an addition to it. Under the supervision of the Franciscan fathers, the Indians built the pueblo mission churches, using the same materials and many of the design concepts they had used for centuries in their own homes. Thus, the Indians' earliest contribution to Christian art was in the

eine unendliche Vielfalt an Interpretationen. Es ist ein Thema, das Menschen auf der ganzen Welt seit zweitausend Jahren fasziniert, und es zeigt auch heute kaum ein Schwinden seiner Anziehungskraft. Gegenwärtig gibt es in Europa hunderte von Mitgliedern der Internationalen Vereinigung der Krippenfreunde, mit dem Hauptsitz in Rom und Zweigstellen in der Bundesrepublik, Österreich und Frankreich.[6] Die Tradition lebt noch stark in Spanien, Mexiko und Südamerika.

Es ist ein eigenartiger Zufall, daß gerade zu der Zeit, als die freistehenden Krippenfiguren in Europa populär wurden, auch die Indianer im Südwesten in erste Berührung mit Europäern kamen und damit auch mit den Symbolen und Kunstformen der christlichen Religion. Als im Jahre 1540 die erste Expedition der spanischen Entdecker in das Gebiet des heutigen Südwestens der Vereinigten Staaten kam, da hatten die Pueblo-Indianer bereits ihre eigene Religion und hoch entwickelte Kunstformen, besonders die Töpferei.[7] Die folgenden 300 Jahre europäischer Herrschaft brachten manche Änderungen in der Lebensweise der Indianer. Am Ende nahmen die meisten das Christentum an, nicht um ihre eigene Religion zu ersetzen, sondern viel mehr als eine Erweiterung derselben. Unter der Leitung der Franziskanerpater bauten die Indianer die Pueblo-Missionskirchen, wobei sie die gleichen Materialien und Bauformen benützten, die sie jahrhundertelang für ihre eigenen Häuser verwendet hatten. So bestand der erste indianische Beitrag zur christlichen Kunst in der

artista, proporcionando una variedad infinita de interpretaciones. Este es un tema que ha cautivado el interés de la población mundial por más de 2,000 años y que no da señales de disminuir. La Asociación de Amigos de la Cuna, en Europa, cuenta con cientos de miembros, y sus oficinas centrales se encuentran en Roma con sucursales en Alemania Occidental, Austria, y Francia.[6] En España, así como en México y América del Sur, la tradición también se encuentra muy arraigada.

De particular singularidad es el hecho que casi al mismo tiempo que los Nacimientos con figuras de bulto empezaron a florecer en Europa, los indios del Suroeste tenían su primer contacto con los europeos y, consecuentemente, con los símbolos y formas de arte de la religión Cristiana. En 1540, cuando la primera expedición de exploradores españoles hizo su entrada en lo que ahora es el suroeste de los Estados Unidos, los indios Pueblo ya tenían su propia religión así como también sus propias formas de arte muy bien desarrolladas, particularmente la de la cerámica.[7] Los 300 años de dominación europea que siguieron trajeron cambios numerosos en las costumbres de los indios. Eventualmente, la mayoría aceptó la religión Católica, no como una suplantación de su religión, pero como un agregado a ésta. Bajo la vigilancia de los padres Franciscanos, los indios construyeron las iglesias y misiones de los pueblos, empleando los mismos materiales y muchos de los diseños y conceptos que por siglos habían empleado en la construcción de sus propios casas. De esa manera la primera contribución de arte de los indios fue en la

architecture of the churches. As one writer has noted, however, "Rarely was the Pueblo artist trusted to portray the saints in pigment or wood."[8] This was originally the province of the padres. Beginning around 1750, much of the religious art for churches and homes was made by Hispanic-American Santeros. They made the Santos — images of Christ, the Holy Family, and saints popular in the region — either carved of wood in the round or painted on wood panels or animal hides.[9] A noted collector has observed: "The Santos of the American Southwest are the only religious art historically derived from American tradition that America can call a part of its own heritage."[10] With the coming of the railroad in the 1880s, however, religious articles could be imported from church shops in the eastern United States, and by 1907 the Santero period had seriously declined.[11]

The railroad also had a tremendous impact on Indian art. It brought the first large wave of tourists, and many potters turned to making objects that appealed to the tourist trade. Cochiti Pueblo, which had a long tradition of figurative pottery, created large figures of padres, cowboys, businessmen, and tourists. Tesuque produced thousands of Rain God figurines, believed to have

Architektur der Kirchen. Jedoch, wie ein Geschichtsschreiber berichtet, "schenkte man dem einheimischen Pueblo-Künstler sehr selten das Vertrauen, die Heiligen in Farbe oder Holz darzustellen."[8] Das war ursprünglich den Priestern vorbehalten, aber um 1750 begann die Zeit der spanisch-amerikanischen *Santeros*, die bald den Großteil der religiösen Kunst für Kirche und Heim anfertigten. Sie schufen die *Santos*-Darstellungen von Christus, der Heiligen Familie, von in ihren Gegenden populären Heiligen, entweder dreidimensional aus Holz geschnitzt oder auf Holztafeln oder Häute gemalt.[9] Ein bekannter Sammler bemerkt dazu: "Die *Santos* des amerikanischen Südwestens sind die einzige religiöse Kunstform, die historisch aus amerikanischer Tradition gewachsen ist, die Amerika als Teil seines eigenen Erbes beanspruchen kann."[10] Jedoch konnten mit dem Eintreffen der Eisenbahn in den 1880er Jahren religiöse Artikel von den Devotionalienhändlern im Osten der Vereinigten Staaten importiert werden, und um 1907 war die *Santero* Produktion stark abgefallen.[11]

Das Kommen der Eisenbahn hatte auch einen äußerst starken Einfluß auf die indianische Kunst. Die Bahn brachte die erste große Touristenwelle, und viele Töpfer wechselten dazu über, Gegenstände zu machen, die den Touristenhandel ansprachen. Das Cochiti Pueblo, das eine alte Tradition in figurativer Töpferei hatte, produzierte jetzt große Figuren von Priestern, Cowboys, Geschäftsleuten und Touristen. Tesuque produzierte Tausende von Regengottstatuetten, von denen man annimmt, daß sie auf alten

arquitectura de las iglesias. Sin embargo, como ha notado un escritor, "era raro que al artista del Pueblo se le confiara la representación de los santos en pintura o hechos de madera."[8] Esto era la provincia de los padres, originalmente. Comenzando a cerca de 1750, mucho del arte religioso en las iglesias y casas fue producto de los Santeros hispanoamericanos, quienes hicieron los Santos — imágenes de Cristo, la Sagrada Familia, y los santos populares en la región — ya sea que estuvieran tallados en madera o pintados en tablones o cueros de animales.[9] Un coleccionista famoso ha dicho que: "Los Santos del Suroeste americano representan el único arte religioso histórico derivado de la tradición americana, lo que América puede llamar su propia herencia."[10] Con la llegada del ferrocarril en 1880, sin embargo, se pudieron importar artículos religiosos de las tiendas de las iglesias en la región oriental de Estados Unidos, y para 1907 la época del Santero había declinado notablemente.[11]

El ferrocarril también tuvo un impacto tremendo en el arte indio. Este trajo los primeros contingentes de turistas, y muchos ceremistas cambiaron sus temas por la creación de objetos que más llamaban la atención de los turistas. El pueblo Cochiti, que por largo tiempo tuvo la tradición de cerámica figurativa, empezó a hacer figuras grandes de padres, vaqueros, hombres de negocios, y turistas. Tesuque produjo miles de figuras del Dios de la Lluvia, que se cree estaban basadas en figuras antiguas. El

been based on ancient figures. Santa Clara Pueblo became noted for its small pottery animals called *animalitos*.[12] These three pueblos were the earliest to make Nativities and still produce the largest number of them. Thus it could be assumed that the fashioning of figures for tourists led to the creation of Nacimientos, but it does not explain the lapse of almost eighty years between the beginning of the tourist period in the 1880s and the emergence of Indian-made Nativities in the late 1950s. One Nativity artisan, Ethel Shields of Acoma, notes that her mother made some Nativity figures around fifty years ago, although not complete sets. There were a number of Hispanic-American woodcarvers doing religious themes, including Nativities, from the first half of the 1900s to the present time.[13] Though their work is completely individual, they could be considered heirs to the Santero tradition. A number of collectors who now have Indian-made Nativities began their collections with the Hispanic-American wood sets. None of the Indian artisans has mentioned these early expressions in their region as having inspired them to do Nativities, but it is possible that the Hispanic-American sets inspired collectors to seek out and encourage Indian-made Nativities.

Two Santa Fe collectors who are known to have provided great impetus are Alexander Girard, a noted designer

Vorbildern beruhen. Santa Clara Pueblo wurde bekannt wegen seiner kleinen Tontiere, *animalitos* genannt.[12] Diese drei Pueblos waren auch die ersten, die Krippen machten, und sie produzieren immer noch die größte Zahl davon. Man könnte also annehmen, daß die Herstellung von Figuren für die Touristen zum Entstehen der *Nacimientos* geführt hat, aber diese Theorie kann nicht erklären, warum beinahe 80 Jahre zwischen dem Beginn der Touristenzeit und dem Auftreten der von Indianern gefertigten Krippen in den 1950er Jahren vergingen. Eine Krippenbildnerin, Ethel Shields von Acoma, bemerkt, daß ihre Mutter vor etwa fünfzig Jahren einige Krippen-figuren machte, allerdings keine vollständigen Gruppen. Es gibt einige spanisch-amerikanische Holzschnitzer, die seit der ersten Hälfte der 1900er Jahre bis heute religiöse Motive darstellen, darunter auch Krippen-szenen.[13] Obwohl ihre Arbeiten total individuell sind, könnte man sie doch als Erben der *Santero* Tradition bezeichnen. Mehrere Sammler, die jetzt indianische Krippen besitzen, begannen ihre Kollektion mit diesen spanisch-amerikanischen holzgeschnitz-ten Krippen. Keiner der indianischen Kunsthandwerker hat diese frühen Krippen als Vorbild erwähnt, es ist jedoch möglich, daß die spanisch-amerikanischen Gruppen ein Ansporn für die Sammler waren, nach india-nischen Krippen zu suchen und deren Produktion zu fördern.

Zwei Sammler aus Santa Fe haben sich als Förderer dieser Kunst besonders verdient gemacht: Alexander Girard, ein bekannter Graphiker und Architekt,

pueblo Santa Clara se dio a conocer por la cerámica de pequeñas figuras de ani-malitos.[12] Estos tres pueblos fueron los primeros que hicieron Nacimientos, y en la actualidad son los que producen el mayor número de ellos. De allí se puede presumir que las figuras modeladas para los turistas llevó a la creación de los Nacimientos, pero esto no explica el lapso de tiempo de casi ochenta años entre el primer período turístico en 1880 y la emergencia de los Nacimientos cre-ados por los indios hasta los últimos años de la década de 1950. Ethel Shields, arte-sana de Acoma, dice que su madre hizo algunas figuras de Nacimiento aproxima-damente hace cincuenta años, aunque nunca hizo juegos completos. Hubo un grupo numeroso de talladores hispano-americanos que se dedicaba a temas religiosos, incluyendo los Nacimientos, desde la primera mitad de 1900 a la fecha.[13] Aunque su trabajo es completa-mente individual, se les puede considerar como a los herederos de la tradición del Santero. Algunos coleccionistas que ahora poseen colecciones hechas por indios empezaron a adquirir con los juegos de madera creados por los artis-tas hispanoamericanos. Ninguno de los artesanos indios ha mencionado que estas primeras expresiones de arte en su región hayan sido la influencia que los inspiró en la creación de sus Nacimien-tos, pero puede ser posible que los juegos de los artistas hispanoamericanos hayan inspirado a los coleccionistas a adquirir y buscar los Nacimientos hechos por los artistas indios.

Dos coleccionistas de Santa Fe que son conocidos por haber inyectado grandes estímulos en la producción de Nacimientos son Alexander Girard,

Detail / Einzelheit / Detalle from Nacimiento
by Maria I. Naranjo (see page 75)

Detail / Einzelheit / Detalle from Nacimiento
by Domingo and Chepa Franco (see page 59)

Detail / Einzelheit / Detalle from Nacimiento
by Manuel Vigil (see page 19)

8

and architect who had one of the largest private folk art collections in the country, and Sallie R. Wagner, who had worked in the Indian arts field for years and had many friends among Indian artisans. As she notes: "Alexander Girard suggested that I encourage the Indians I knew to make Nacimientos. He wanted to encourage good things, particularly among the lesser-known artists." This resulted in Manuel Vigil's entering the field, as well as his daughter, Anna Marie. Perhaps the greatest impetus came in December 1961 with the exhibit of the Girard collection of Nativities at the Museum of International Folk Art in Santa Fe. Among the 124 items featured, representing more than twenty countries, were two Indian-made Nativities, a painted pottery set by Anna Marie Vigil (now Lovato) of Tesuque and a carved wood set by Pete Aguino of San Juan Pueblo. The exhibit created an interest in the theme among collectors and may have, at least indirectly, inspired Indian artisans. *New Mexico* magazine reported in its December 1962 issue: "Perhaps the most dramatic and colorful exhibit ever presented at the Museum of International Folk Art in Santa Fe was the Nacimiento display during the Christmas season last year and repeated in part this year." From November 1962 to January 1963, Hallmark Cards sponsored a huge exhibit of the Girard Nativity collection

der eine der größten Privatsammlungen im Lande besaß, und Sallie R. Wagner, die viele Jahre auf dem Gebiet der Indianerkunst tätig war und viele Freunde unter den indianischen Kunstgewerblern hatte. Sie schreibt: "Alexander Girard schlug mir vor, daß ich mir bekannte Indianer ermuntern sollte, *Nacimientos* zu fertigen. Er wollte besonders bei weniger bekannten Künstlern die Herstellung von hoher Qualität fördern." Als Folge davon begannen Manuel Vigil und seine Tochter Anna Marie auf diesem Gebiet zu arbeiten. Den größten Ansporn gab wahrscheinlich die Ausstellung der Girard Krippensammlung in Dezember 1961, im Museum für Internationale Volkskunst in Santa Fe. Unter den 124 Ausstellungsgegenständen, die mehr als zwanzig Länder repräsentierten, waren zwei von Indianern gefertigte Krippen, eine bemalte Tongruppe von Anna Marie Vigil (jetzt Lovato) aus Tesuque, und eine geschnitzte Holzgruppe von Pete Aguino aus dem San Juan Pueblo. Diese Ausstellung erweckte das Interesse anderer Sammler am Krippen-motiv, und sie mag, zumindest indirekt, die indianischen Künstler inspiriert haben. Das Magazin *New Mexico* berichtete in seiner Ausgabe vom Dezember 1962: "Die vielleicht dramatischste und farbigste Ausstellung, die je vom Museum für Internationale Volkskunst in Santa Fe veranstaltet wurde, war die vorjährige weihnacht-liche *Nacimiento* Ausstellung, die dieses Jahr teilweise wiederholt wurde." Vom November 1962 bis Januar 1963 veranstaltete die Firma Hallmark Grußkarten eine große Ausstellung der Girard Krippenkollektion (170 Gruppen)

famoso diseñanador y arquitecto que poseía una de las colecciones privadas de arte folklórico más grandes en todo el país, y Sallie R. Wagner, que había tra-bajado en el campo artístico de los indios por muchos años y contaba con numero-sos amigos entre los artesanos indios. Como ella comenta: "Alexander Girard sugirió que yo había animado a los indios que yo conocía a que hicieran Nacimientos. El quería patrocinar cosas buenas, particularmente entre los artistas menos conocidos." Este fue el resultado de que Manuel Vigil entrara en este campo al igual que lo hizo su hija Anna Marie. Posiblemente el mayor impulso vino en diciembre de 1961 con la exhi-bición de los Nacimientos de Girard en el Museo de Arte Folklórico Interna-cional en Santa Fe. Dentro de los 124 artículos expuestos, representando a más de veinte países, se encontraban dos Nacimientos de artistas indios: un juego de cerámica pintado por Anna Marie Vigil (ahora Lovato) de Tesuque y un juego tallado en madera, creación de Pete Aguina del pueblo San Juan. La exhibición despertó el interés de los coleccionistas en el tema y también hizo que, indirectamente, los artistas indios se inspiraran en el. La revista *New Mexico*, en su número de diciembre de 1962, hizo el siguiente comentario: "Posiblemente la exhibición más dramá-tica y colorida que jamás haya presen-tado el Museo de Arte Folklórico Inter-nacional fue la de los Nacimientos en la temporada de Navidad el año pasado y que este año se está repitiendo en parte." De noviembre de 1962 a enero de 1963, Hallmark Cards patrocinó una gran exhi-bición de la Colección de Nacimientos de Girard (170 escenas) en una galería

(170 scenes) at a gallery in Kansas City, Missouri, which established new attendance records. Twelve color reproductions from the exhibit were featured in the Hallmark Nativity Calendar for 1963.

Indian artisans also had long exposure to the Nativities in their mission churches, most of them commercial imports. As Maria I. Naranjo of Santa Clara said, "I never dreamed of making one for the church. We always had the Italian style." Nevertheless, her admiration of the church set inspired her to make her first Nativity. In the early 1960s Father Camillus Cavagnaro on the Papago reservation commissioned Domingo and Chepa Franco to make a Nativity for San Jose Mission church. In 1965 Cristo Rey Church in Santa Fe commissioned Manuel Vigil to do one of his Pueblo-style sets. Other sets of his are in Saint Francis Cathedral in Santa Fe and in many Catholic churches in Albuquerque. In the 1970s his were the first Indian Nativities to be displayed in the Pueblo mission churches.

Several museums also played an important role in the Nacimiento movement. The Museum of New Mexico Foundation asked Maria I. Naranjo to make a set (her second) for the opening of their new shop in 1965. That same year the Arizona State Museum in Tucson commissioned the Francos to do a Nativity for their permanent collection. The Museum of International Folk

in einer Kunstgalerie in Kansas City, Missouri, die neue Rekordzahlen an Besuchern brachte. Zwölf farbige Reproduktionen erschienen im Hallmark Weihnachtskrippen-Kalender für das Jahr 1963.

Indianische Kunstgewerbler hatten natürlich schon lange in ihren Missionskirchen Krippen gesehen, meist importierte Massenware. Wie es Maria I. Naranjo aus Santa Clara ausdrückt: "Ich dachte nie im Traume daran, eine für die Kirche zu machen. Wir hatten immer die im italienischen Stil." Und doch inspirierte sie ihre Bewunderung der Kirchenkrippe dazu, ihre erste eigene Krippe zu machen. Anfangs der 1960er Jahre beauftragte Pater Camillus Cavagnaro auf der Papago Reservation das Ehepaar Domingo und Chepa Franco, eine Krippe für die Missionskirche San Jose zu machen. Im Jahre 1965 bestellte die Cristo Rey Kirche in Santa Fe von Manuel Vigil eine seiner Krippen im Pueblo-Stil. Andere seiner Krippen sind jetzt in der St. Francis Kathedrale in Santa Fe und in vielen katholischen Kirchen in Albuquerque. Seine Krippen waren es, die in den 1970er Jahren als erste indianische Krippen in den Pueblo Missionskirchen aufgestellt wurden.

Mehrere Museen spielten ebenfalls eine wichtige Rolle in der *Nacimiento* Bewegung. Die Stiftung des Museums von New Mexico bestellte von Maria I. Naranjo eine Krippe (ihre zweite) für die Eröffnung des neuen Verkaufsräumes im Jahre 1965. Im selben Jahr gab das Arizona State Museum in Tucson einen Auftrag an die Francos, eine Krippe für die ständige Kollektion zu liefern. Das Museum für Interna-

de Kansas City, Missouri, la que estableció una nueva marca de asistencia. Doce reproducciones de la exhibición, a todo color, caracterizaron un calendario de 1963 de Hallmark.

Los artistas indios también estuvieron expuestos a los Nacimientos en sus iglesias, aunque la mayoría de ellos eran importaciones comerciales. Como dijo María I. Naranjo del pueblo Santa Clara: "Nunca soñé en hacer uno para la iglesia. Siempre teníamos los de estilo italiano." No obstante, su admiración por el juego de la iglesia fue la que la inspiró a que hiciera su primer Nacimiento. A principios de 1960 el padre Camillus Cavagnaro de la Reservación Pápago comisionó a Domingo y Chepa Franco para que hicieran un Nacimiento para la Iglesia de San José. En 1965 la Iglesia de Cristo Rey en Santa Fe comisionó a Manuel Vigil para que hiciera uno de sus juegos al estilo "Pueblo." Otros de sus juegos se encuentran en la Catedral de San Francisco en Santa Fe y en muchas de las Iglesias Católicas de Albuquerque. En 1970 los juegos de Vigil fueron los primeros Nacimientos indios que se exhibieron en las iglesias misioneras de los pueblos.

Algunos museos también jugaron un papel importante en el movimiento de los Nacimientos. La Fundación del Museo de Nuevo México pidió a María I. Naranjo que hiciera un juego (su segundo) con motivo de la apertura de la tienda nueva del museo. Ese mismo año el Museo del Estado de Arizona comisionó a los Franco la creación de un Nacimiento para su colección permanente. En los últimos años el Museo de

Art has commissioned many sets over the years and often displays them at Christmas. A new wing is now under construction at the museum to house the Girard Foundation collection, which he donated in 1978, insuring even more extensive displays in the future.

Indian-oriented art galleries and shops have also commissioned Indian artisans to do sets since the 1960s, originally for display only at Christmas. Now, however, a number of them, including shops run by the Museum of New Mexico Foundation and the Museum of Northern Arizona, display and sell them year-round. A gallery in Denver has held juried shows for Indian-made Nativities the weekend before Thanksgiving each year since 1974. A gallery in Albuquerque is planning a Nativities exhibit in the fall of 1979.

Thus, the earliest impetus for the making of Nativities among southwest Indian artists came from major collectors, the Catholic church, museums, shops, and galleries. But the movement could not have swelled to its present proportions without the interest and demand of the public. Several other movements could have made an impact at just this point. The civil rights movement of the 1960s changed attitudes and opened

tionale Volkskunst hat während der vergangenen Jahre viele Aufträge vergeben, und stellt diese Krippen oft während der Weihnachtszeit aus. Gegenwärtig wird ein neuer Flügel gebaut, der die von Girard im Jahre 1978 gestiftete Sammlung behausen wird und so für die Zukunft eine noch umfangreichere Ausstellung von Krippen gewährleistet.

Die an indianischen Arbeiten interessierten Galerien und Geschäfte haben seit den 1960er Jahren ebenfalls Krippenaufträge an indianische Kunsthandwerker vergeben. Ursprünglich wurden diese Krippen nur zur Weihnachtszeit ausgestellt, aber jetzt zeigen und verkaufen viele Aussteller, darunter die Verkaufsräume der Stiftung des Museums von New Mexico und des Museums von Northern Arizona, ihre Krippen das ganze Jahr hindurch. Eine Galerie in Denver hält seit 1974 an den Wochenenden vor *Thanksgiving* eine Ausstellung ausgewählter indianischer Krippen ab, und eine Galerie in Albuquerque plant eine Krippenausstellung für den Herbst 1979.

So waren es die großen Sammler, die katholische Kirche, Museen, Kunstgéwerbeläden und Galerien, die als erste die indianischen Künstler des Südwestens zur Anfertigung von Krippen ermunterten. Aber diese Bewegung hätte nicht auf ihr gegenwärtiges Ausmaß anwachsen können, ohne das Interesse und die Nachfrage der Öffentlichkeit zu besitzen. Es mag auch sein, daß gerade zu jener Zeit andere Bewegungen einen Einfluß ausübten. Die Bürgerrechtsbewegung der sechziger Jahre veränderte alte Einstellungen und öffnete neue Tore für die

Arte Folklórico Internacional ha encargado numerosos juegos y en tiempo de Navidad presenta varias exhibiciones. Actualmente el museo está construyendo una nueva ala, la cual albergará la Colección de la Fundación Girard que él donó en 1978, asegurando de esta manera exhibiciones más extensas para el futuro.

Desde 1960, las galerías y tiendas de arte indio han comisionado a artesanos indios en la creación de Nacimientos, originalmente para exhibirlas en Navidad únicamente. Sin embargo, en la actualidad un número de tiendas, incluyendo las de la Fundación del Museo de Nuevo México y la del Museo del Norte de Arizona, exhiben y venden los Nacimientos durante todo el año. Una galería en Denver, desde 1974, ha llevado a cabo exhibiciones con jurado calificador durante el fin de semana anterior al Día de Dar Gracias para los Nacimientos hechos por artistas indios. Una galería de Albuquerque está planeando una exhibición de Nacimientos para el otoño de 1979.

Así, los primeros estímulos para la creación de Nacimientos entre los artistas indios del Suroeste vinieron de los principales coleccionistas, de la Iglesia Católica, y de los museos, tiendas, y galerías. Pero el movimiento no podría haber crecido a sus proporciones actuales sin que hubiera existido la demanda e interés del público. Pudiera ser también que algunos otros movimientos hayan hecho cierto impacto precisamente en este punto. El movimiento de los

new doors to minorities. Exactly coinciding with this was the surge in the charismatic movement of the churches, which ushered in a new ecumenicalism and liberalism, and this was felt in the small mission churches in the pueblos and reservations. For instance, one of the Nativity artisans, Dorothy Trujillo of Cochiti, and her husband Onofre are active in the charismatic movement and have attended conferences at Notre Dame University, Indiana, in California, and other parts of the country. Several other artisans are active in outreach groups of the church.

Although the Indian Nativity artisans are relative newcomers to the Christian art field, they are the only large homogeneous group in the United States now known to be producing art on a single Christian theme. In fact, other than the Santeros, this country has not had any indigenous groups of artists in the Christian art tradition. Perhaps one day the Indian Nativity artisans of the Southwest may become as well-known as the great Nativity artists of Europe — the *santonniers* of Provence, the woodcarvers of Oberammergau, the *figurari* of Naples, and the *pesebristas* of Spain.

Minoritäten. Gleichzeitig erlebten die Kirchen ein Anschwellen der charismatischen Strömung, die eine neue ökumenische und liberale Bewegung mit sich brachte, was in den kleinen Missionskirchen in den Pueblos und Reservaten seinen Niederschlag fand. So ist zum Beispiel die Krippenbildnerin Dorothy Trujillo von Cochiti zusammen mit ihrem Mann Onofre in der charismatischen Bewegung tätig, und sie haben an Tagungen an der Notre Dame Universität in Indiana, in Kalifornien und anderen Teilen des Landes teilgenommen. Manche andere Künstler sind im Hilfswerk ihrer Kirche aktiv.

Obwohl die indianischen Krippenbildner relative Neulinge auf dem Gebiet der christlichen Kunst sind, stellen sie doch gegenwärtig die einzige bekannte homogene Gruppe von Künstlern dar, die sich in den Vereinigten Staaten mit nur einem gemeinsamen christlichen Thema beschäftigen. Tatsächlich haben die Vereinigten Staaten, mit Ausnahme der *Santeros*, noch nie einheimische Künstlergruppen in der Tradition der christlichen Kunst gehabt. Vielleicht werden eines Tages die indianischen Krippenmacher des Südwestens so berühmt werden wie die großen Krippenkünstler Europas: die *santonniers* der Provence, die Holzschnitzer von Oberammergau, die *figurari* von Neapel und die *pesebristas* aus Spanien.

Derechos Civiles en 1960 cambió actitudes y abrió nuevas puertas a las minorías. Coincidiendo exactamente con esto fue el surgimiento del movimiento carismático en las iglesias, el cual pugnó por más ecumeniquismo y liberalismo, y esto se notó en las pequeñas iglesias misioneras de los pueblos y reservaciones. Por ejemplo, una de las artistas de Nacimientos, Dorothy Trujillo, y su esposo Onofre, son participantes activos del movimiento carismático y han asistido a conferencias en la Universidad Notre Dame, en Indiana, en California, y en otras partes del país. Algunos artistas más también participan en los grupos locales de sus iglesias.

Aunque los artesanos indios que son creadores de Nacimientos son relativamente nuevos en el campo de arte Cristiano, representan el único grupo numeroso y homogéneo en los Estados Unidos que es conocido por su producción de arte de un solo tema Cristiano. En realidad, aparte de los Santeros, este país no ha contado con ningún grupo de artistas indígenas dedicado a la tradición del arte Cristiano. Tal vez con el tiempo los artistas indios del Suroeste que son creadores de Nacimientos lleguen a ser tan bien conocidos como los artistas europeos — los *santonniers* de Provenza, los talladores de madera de Oberammergau, los *figurai* de Nápoles, y los *pesebristas* de España.

MANUEL VIGIL made his first Nacimiento twenty years ago and thus is the first southwest Indian artisan to turn to this art form. But it is not only longevity that qualifies him as dean of southwest Indian Nativity artisans, but his tremendous versatility and productivity. He estimates that between 1964 and 1977 he made between 1,000 and 2,000 sets. Yet despite this huge production, each set is individual. His versatility is evident in the fact that he does five distinct styles — the Colonial painted figures, Colonial cloth-clothed figures, the Pueblo Indian, the Plains Indian, and the simple, unadorned micaceous clay figures. Within each of the first four styles there is a wide range of interpretations and variations. Also, in contrast to other pueblo artisans who work solely in clay, he incorporates many other materials with his clay figures. His technique, too, differs from other pueblo potters in that the figures are painted *after* firing, a characteristic of much of Tesuque's pottery. Another characteristic typical of his pueblo is his modeling of faces, particularly the large, bridgeless noses that descend in a straight line from the forehead. This is a consistent

MANUEL VIGIL schuf seine erste Weihnachtskrippe vor zwanzig Jahren und ist somit der erste indianische Kunsthandwerker des Südwestens, der sich dieser Kunstform zugewandt hat. Es ist aber nicht nur seine Langlebigkeit, die ihn zum führenden Vertreter der südwestindianischen Weihnachtskrippenhersteller macht, sondern auch seine enorme Vielseitigkeit und Produktivität. Nach seiner eigenen Schätzung hat er von 1964 bis 1977 zwischen 1000 und 2000 Gruppen hergestellt. Trotz dieser gewaltigen Produktion ist aber jede Gruppe individuell. Seine Vielseitigkeit zeigt sich in der Tatsache, daß er Figuren in fünf verschiedenen Stilen anfertigt: die bemalten Figuren im Kolonialstil, koloniale in Tuch gekleidete Figuren, den Puebloindianer, den Prärieindianer und die einfachen, unverzierten Figuren aus glimmerhaltigem Ton. Innerhalb der ersten vier Stile gibt es vielerlei Interpretationen und Variationen. Im Gegensatz zu anderen Pueblo-Kunsthandwerkern, die ausschließlich mit Ton arbeiten, verbindet er viele andere Materialien mit seinen Tonfiguren. Auch seine Methode unterscheidet sich von anderen Pueblo-Töpfern: seine Gestalten werden erst *nach* dem Brennen bemalt — ein Merkmal, das die meisten keramischen Erzeugnisse Tesuques kennzeichnet. Ein weiteres Merkmal, das für sein Pueblo typisch ist, ist die Modellierung der Gesichter, insbesondere die großen, rückenlosen Nasen, die von der Stirne in einer geraden Linie nach unten laufen. Dies ist ein unfehl-

MANUEL VIGIL creó su primer Nacimiento hace veinte años, y así es el primer artista indio que participó en esta forma de arte. Sin embargo, no es por haber sido el primero en este campo que lo clasifican como "decano" de los artistas indios del Suroeste que crean Nacimientos, sino también por la versatilidad de su obra y por su rendimiento tremendo. Vigil calcula que creó de 1,000 a 2,000 juegos entre los años 1964 y 1977. A pesar de esta obra enorme, cada juego es único. Su versatilidad se muestra en los cinco estilos distintos que emplea: figuras pintadas al estilo Colonial, figuras con trajes de tela del mismo estilo Colonial, el Indio Pueblo, el Indio Plains, y las figuras sencillas y sin adornar de arcilla micácea. Dentro de cada uno de los primer cuatro estilos hay una gran diversidad de innovaciones y de variaciones. En contraste con otros artistas del pueblo indio que emplean solamente arcilla, Vigil emplea varios otros materiales para su obra. El método que usa también se distingue de los otros ceramistas del pueblo indio, porque el pinta las figuras *después* de cocerlas al fuego, una característica de mucho de la cerámica de Tesuque. Un otro característica típica de su pueblo es cómo modela las caras, en particular las narices grandes sin caballete, que descienden en una línea directa de la frente. Esta aparece consistentemente en las figuras

feature of the Tesuque Rain God figurines for which the pueblo has long been noted.

Vigil was born on June 10, 1900, in Tesuque Pueblo. His mother, Anastasia Vigil, was a potter and made the Rain God figurines. Vigil recalls, "When I was six or seven years old I would sit by her side and watch her make pottery. Then I started working in clay, too." He attended Saint Catherine's School in Santa Fe until the fourth grade and later went into farming. He was noted as a dancer, taking part in all of the pueblo's ceremonial dances, and at one time gave dance demonstrations in Wisconsin and New York. Then in 1948 he was struck by a car in a hit-and-run accident that broke one leg and necessitated amputation of the other. During the long months in the hospital he began doing beadwork and, later, moccasins and drums. Since he could no longer do farm work, he joined his wife, Vicenta, in making pottery. It was the beginning of a lifelong collaboration. Manuel does the modeling and sanding of the figures; Vicenta does the firing and most of the painting, as well as making the clothes and accessories. The couple have four daughters and an adopted son. All of the girls are active in the arts. Their second daughter, Anna Marie Lovato, is also one of the earliest Indian artists to do Nativity scenes.

Among Vigil's earliest figures were Indian ceremonial dancers. He says,

bares Kennzeichen der Tesuque-Regengottstatuetten, für die das Pueblo schon seit langem bekannt ist.

Vigil wurde am 10. Juni 1900 in Tesuque-Pueblo geboren. Seine Mutter Anastasia Vigil war eine Töpferin und fertigte die Regengottstatuetten an. Vigil erinnert sich: "Als ich sechs oder sieben Jahre alt war, saß ich neben ihr und sah zu, wie sie Töpferwaren anfertigte. Dann fing auch ich an, Ton zu bearbeiten." Er besuchte die Grund-schule der Heiligen Katharina in Santa Fe bis zur vierten Klasse, und später betrieb er Landwirtschaft. Er war als Tänzer bekannt, nahm an allen zeremo-niellen Tänzen des Pueblos teil, und demonstrierte einmal Indianertänze in Wisconsin und New York. Dann wurde er 1948 bei einem Unfall mit Fahrer-flucht von einem Wagen angefahren; eines seiner Beine wurde gebrochen, das andere mußte amputiert werden. Während der langen Monate im Krankenhaus fing er an, Perlenstickerei zu machen, und später fertigte er Mokassins und Trommeln an. Da er nicht länger in der Landwirtschaft arbeiten konnte, half er seiner Frau Vicenta beim Töpfern. Das war der Anfang einer lebenslänglichen Zusam-menarbeit. Manuel modelliert die Gestalten und schmirgelt sie ab. Vicenta brennt und bemalt sie und stellt die Kleidung und Zubehör her. Das Ehepaar hat vier Töchter und einen adoptierten Sohn. Die Töchter sind alle aktive Künstlerinnen, und die zweite Tochter, Anna Marie Lovato, ist auch eine der ersten indianischen Künstlerinnen, die Weihnachtskrippen angefertigt hat.

Unter Vigils frühesten Gestalten waren indianische Zeremonientänzer.

de "Dios de la Lluvia" del pueblo Tesuque, por las cuales el pueblo es conocido desde muchos años.

Vigil nació el 10 de julio de 1900, en el pueblo Tesuque. Su madre, Anastasia Vigil, también ceramista, creó las figuras de "Dios de la Lluvia." Vigil nos cuenta: "Cuando tenía seis o siete años me sen-taba a su lado y miraba cómo creaba cerámica. Entonces, yo también comencé a trabajar con arcilla." Asistió a la Escuela de Santa Catalina en Santa Fe hasta el cuarto grado y luego comenzó a trabajar en la agricultura. Fue un dan-zarín conocido y participaba en todas las danzas ceremoniales de su pueblo. Durante esa época dio demostraciones de baile en Wisconsin y en Nueva York. En 1948 tuvo un accidente en el cual un automóvil lo arrolló y el conductor se dio a la fuga. Se rompió una pierna y fue necesario amputarle la otra. Tuvo que pasar muchos meses en el hospital, y durante este tiempo creó por primera vez artículos de cuentas y luego moca-sines y tambores. Como ya no podía hacer el trabajo de agricultor, colaboró con su esposa en la fabricación de cerámica. Así comenzó el trabajo colec-tivo que dura todavía. Manuel modela y lija las figuras; Vicenta se ocupa de cocer al fuego y en la mayor parte del pintado, así como de las ropas y accesso-rios. Los dos tienen cuatro hijas y un hijo adoptivo. Todas las hijas participan en las artes. La segunda de ellas, llamada Anna Marie Lovato, fue una de las primeras artistas en crear Nacimientos.

Entre las primeras figuras de Vigil se encuentran indios que toman parte en

"Those first figures were crude and the family laughed at them, but then they won First Prize at the Santa Fe Indian Market." He also did other scenes of pueblo life, and in the early 1950s he began dealing with Christian themes, doing clay interpretations of the Virgin of Guadalupe and the Crucifixion. Around 1959, at the suggestion of Sallie R. Wagner, he made his first Nativity. It was the painted Colonial style. Several years later he did the Pueblo and Plains Indian styles, and last, the micaceous clay. Vicenta notes: "At first we did a few sets just before Christmas each year; now we work on them year-round." They make settings and wood stables and cribs for their Nativities on special order. Vigil's were the first Indian Nativities to be used in many pueblo churches. In 1973 Vigil was the only southwest Indian artist represented in a large exhibition of Nativities from the international collection of Dr. Maria Elisabeth Houtzager, held in Eindhoven, Netherlands.

Er erklärt: "Jene ersten Figuren waren primitiv und die Familie lachte darüber, aber dann gewannen sie den ersten Preis beim Santa Fe-Indianermarkt." Er fertigte auch andere Szenen aus dem Pueblo-Leben an, und am Anfang der fünfziger Jahre fing er an, christliche Themen zu behandeln, indem er Interpretationen der Jungfrau von Guadalupe und der Kreuzigung Christi in Ton gestaltete. Um 1959 folgte er einem Vorschlag Sallie R. Wagners und gestaltete seine erste Weihnachtskrippe im bemalten Kolonialstil. Einige Jahre später arbeitete er im Pueblo- und Prärieindianer-Stil, und schließlich mit glimmerhaltigem Ton. Vicenta bemerkt: "Zuerst machten wir jedes Jahr ganz kurz vor Weihnachten einige Gruppen; jetzt arbeiten wir das ganze Jahr hindurch an ihnen." Auf besondere Bestellung machen sie die szenischen Hintergründe, Holzställe und Kinderbetten für ihre Weihnachtskrippen. Vigils indianische Weihnachtskrippen waren die ersten, die sowohl in vielen Pueblo-Kirchen als auch in den Kirchen von Santa Fe und Albuquerque benutzt wurden. In einer grossen Ausstellung von Weihnachtskrippen aus der internationalen Sammlung Dr. Maria Elisabeth Houtzager, die 1973 in Eindhoven in den Niederlanden abgehalten wurde, war Vigil der einzige Vertreter der südwestlichen Indianerkunsthandwerker.

bailes ceremoniales. Dice: "Esas primeras figuras fueron toscas, y toda la familia se rió de ellas, pero consiguieron el Primer Premio en el Mercado Indio de Santa Fe." También reprodujo otras escenas de la vida del pueblo indio. Poco después de 1950 empezó con obras que trataron sobre temas cristianos, como las interpretaciones en arcilla de la Virgen de Guadalupe y de la Crucifixión. Hacia el año 1959, siguiendo el consejo de Sallie R. Wagner, creó su primer Nacimiento pintado al estilo Colonial. Después de unos años comenzó a emplear los estilos de los Indios Plain y de los Indios Pueblo, y, por fin, empleó la arcilla micácea. Vicenta observa: "Al empezar, hacíamos unos cuantos juegos cada año, sólo antes de la Navidad; ahora los creamos durante todo el año." Manuel y Vicenta hacen escenas y establos de madera y cunas para sus Nacimientos por encargo especial. Los de Vigil fueron los primeros Nacimientos indios que se usaron en muchas de las iglesias de los pueblos indios. En 1973 en la ciudad de Eindhoven de los Países Bajos, Vigil fue el único artista indio del Suroeste representado en una gran exhibición de Nacimientos de la colección internacional de la doctora Maria Elisabeth Houtzager.

MANUEL VIGIL   14-piece set
  2½″ to 9″ high   ca. 1960
This is Vigil's painted Colonial style, featuring
the costumes of early Spanish colonists in
New Mexico. This style is usually shown with
the traditional cross-legged wooden crib. The
large size of the Infant in proportion to the
adults is evident here and is a characteristic of
all Vigil sets. The three shepherds carry a gold
vase, a sheep, and a goose. The ornate robes
and headwear of the Three Wise Men suggest
the hierarchy of the church. They bear
religious objects of gold — an orb, a mirror
(symbol of the Virgin), and a censer. The angels
are dignified and distinctive. Sallie R. Wagner,
Santa Fe, New Mexico.

MANUEL VIGIL   Gruppe von vierzehn
  Figuren   6,4 bis 22,9 cm hoch   ca. 1960
Hier sehen wir Vigils bemalten Kolonialstil,
der die Kostüme der frühen spanischen
Kolonisten in New Mexico anschaulich macht.
Dieser Stil wird gewöhnlich mit der traditionellen Holzkrippe mit gekreuzten Beinen
gezeigt. Die Größe des Kindes im Verhältnis
zu den Erwachsenen ist offensichtlich und ist
ein Charakteristikum aller Gruppen Vigils.
Die drei Hirten tragen eine goldene Vase, ein
Schaf und eine weiße Gans. Die reich
geschmückten Gewänder und der Kopfschmuck
der drei Weisen deuten auf die Hierarchie der
Kirche hin. Sie tragen religiöse Gegenstände
aus Gold — eine Kugel, einen Spiegel (Symbol
der Heiligen Jungfrau) und ein Weihrauchfaß.
Die Engel sind würdig und charaktervoll.
Sallie R. Wagner, Santa Fe, New Mexico.

MANUEL VIGIL   juego de 14 figuras
  de 6.4 cm. a 22.9 cm. de alto   circa 1960
Este es el estilo Colonial en el que pinta Vigil,
del cual se destacan los trajes de los primeros
colonistas españoles en Nuevo México. De
costumbre este estilo incluye la cuna tradicional
con los pies cruzados. El tamaño largo del Niño
Jesús es evidente comparado con el de los
adultos y es una característica en todos los
juegos de Vigil. Los tres pastores traen un vaso
de oro, una oveja, y una oca. Las sotanas
adornadas y los tocados de los Tres Reyes
Magos representan la jerarquía de la iglesia.
Portan artículos religiosos de oro: un orbe, un
espejo (que simboliza la Virgen), y un incen-
sario. Los ángeles son dignificados y distintivos.
Sallie R. Wagner, Santa Fe, Nuevo México.

MANUEL VIGIL   12-piece set
    1½" to 7¼" high   1963
Vigil refers to this as his "Colonial style with
clothes," though it is very different in feeling
from his painted Colonial style. The human
figures and the camel are done in natural color
clay. Vicenta Vigil made the clothes of seersucker, plain cotton, velvet, and felt with
accents of rickrack and sequins. Even the camel
has a lavishly decorated velvet saddle blanket.
Joseph carries a reed staff; the two shepherds
have staffs made of pipe cleaners. International
Folk Art Foundation Collection in the Museum
of New Mexico, Santa Fe. Gift of
Sallie R. Wagner.

MANUEL VIGIL   Gruppe von zwölf Figuren
    3,8 bis 18,4 cm hoch   1963
Vigil bezeichnet diese Gruppe als seinen
"Kolonialstil mit Kleidung", obwohl dieser
sich gefühlsmäßig von seinem bemalten
Kolonialstil sehr unterscheidet. Die Menschen-
gestalten und das Kamel sind aus naturfarbigem
Ton gestaltet. Vicenta Vigil verfertigte die
Kleider aus leichtem kreppartigem Leinen,
Baumwolle, Samt und Filz, und verzierte sie mit
Zickzacklitzen und Ziermünzen. Sogar das
Kamel hat eine überreichlich geschmückte
Satteldecke aus Samt. Josef trägt einen
Rohrstab; die Stäbe der zwei Hirten sind aus
Pfeifenreinigern gemacht. Sammlung der
Internationalen Volkskunst-Stiftung im Museum
von New Mexico in Santa Fe.
Geschenk Sallie R. Wagner.

MANUEL VIGIL   juego de 12 figuras
    de 3.8 cm. a 18.4 cm. de alto   1963
Vigil califica este juego como "estilo Colonial
con ropa," aunque la impresión que da éste sea
muy distinta de las otras obras pintadas al estilo
Colonial. Las figuras humanas y la del camello
son de arcilla de color natural. La ropa hecha
por Vicenta Vigil es de varios tipos de tela
("seersucker," una tela anonadada; algodón;
terciopelo; y fieltro) y está dornada con "rickrack" y lentejuelas. El camello también lleva
una frazada en la silla de terciopelo con orna-
mentación profusa. José trae un bastón de
caña, y los que llevan los dos pastores son de
limpiapipas. Colección de la Fundación de
Arte Folklórico Internacional en el Museo de
Nuevo México, Santa Fe. Obsequio de
Sallie R. Wagner.

MANUEL VIGIL 14-piece set
   2″ to 6½″ high   1975
Vigil's Plains Indian style is, perhaps, the most
startling of all his Nativity styles. Made of
fired clay and painted in brilliant poster colors,
all of the male figures including the Christ
Child wear the aprons and leggings of the
Plains Indian. All have cloth-wrapped braided
hairstyles adorned with feathers. The Three
Wise Men bring gifts — a gourd rattle, medicine
pouch, and a leather shield with a beaded
pattern on one side. The shepherds carry a dog,
sheep, and goose. Museum of Northern Arizona
Shop, Flagstaff, Arizona.

MANUEL VIGIL   Gruppe von vierzehn
   Figuren   5,1 bis 16,5 cm hoch   1975
Vigils Prärieindianer-Stil ist vielleicht der
aufsehenerregendste seiner Nativitätsstile.
Alle aus gebranntem Ton gebildeten und mit
glänzenden Plakatfarben bemalten männlichen
Figuren, einschließlich des Christkindes,
tragen Schürzen und Leggings der Prärieindianer. Alle haben mit Tuch umwickelte und
mit Federn geschmückte Haarflechten. Die
drei Weisen bringen Geschenke — eine Kürbis-
rassel, einen Medizinbeutel und einen Leder-
schild mit einem Perlenmuster auf der einen
Seite. Die Hirten tragen einen Hund, ein Schaf
und eine Gans. Verkaufsstelle des Museums von
Northern Arizona, Flagstaff, Arizona.

MANUEL VIGIL   juego de 14 figuras
   de 5.1 cm. a 16.5 cm. de alto   1975
Su interpretación del estilo de los Indios Plains
es probablemente el más sorprendente de todos
sus estilos de Nacimientos. Las figuras humanas
masculinas, incluso la del Niño Jesús, están
hechas de arcilla cocida a fuego y pintadas en
colores brillantes, y llevan los delantales y las
polainas de los Indios Plains. Todos tienen el
pelo trenzado, envuelto con tela, y adornado
con plumas. Los Tres Reyes Magos traen como
regalos un sonajero de calabaza, una bolsa de
medicamentos, y un escudo de cuero adornado
por un lado con un diseño de abalorios. Los
pastores traen un perro, una oveja, y una oca.
Tienda del Museo de Arizona del Norte en
Flagstaff, Arizona.

MANUEL VIGIL   14-piece set
   2″ to 7″ high   ca. 1963
Another style developed by Vigil for his
Nativity sets are these simple unadorned figures
in micaceous clay. This clay, flecked with tiny
bits of mica, is often used for pottery in the
northern pueblos of New Mexico. After
modeling in conventional clay, Vigil dries and
sands the figures, then applies a slip of
micaceous clay and fires the figures. Their
classic beauty is reminiscent of the prehistoric
Japanese Haniwa, figures set around royal
burial mounds. International Folk Art
Foundation Collection in the Museum of New
Mexico, Santa Fe. Gift of Sallie R. Wagner.

MANUEL VIGIL   Gruppe von vierzehn
   Figuren   5,1 bis 17,8 cm hoch   ca. 1963
Eine andere Stilart, die Vigil für seine
Weihnachtskrippen entwickelt hat, ist die der
einfachen schmucklosen Gestalten aus
glimmerhaltigem Ton. Dieser mit kleinen
Glimmerblättchen gesprenkelte Ton wird oft in
den nördlichen Pueblos von New Mexico für
die Töpferkunst verwendet. Nachdem er mit
herkömmlichem Ton modelliert hat, trocknet
und schmirgelt Vigil die Gestalten ab; dann
trägt er einen geschlämmten Überzug aus
glimmerhaltigem Ton auf und brennt sie. Ihre
klassische Schönheit erinnert an die prähistorischen japanischen *Haniwa*, Figuren, die um
königliche Grabhügel aufgestellt wurden.
Sammlung der Internationalen Volkskunst-
Stiftung im Museum von New Mexico,
Santa Fe. Geschenk Sallie R. Wagner.

MANUEL VIGIL   juego de 14 figuras
   de 5.1 cm. a 17.8 cm. de alto   circa 1963
Estas figuras sencillas y sin adorno, hechas con
arcilla micácea, representan otro estilo de
Nacimiento realizado por Vigil. En los pueblos
indios del norte de Nuevo México se crea
mucha cerámica de esta arcilla con motas de
mica. Primero, Vigil modela las figuras con la
arcilla convencional y luego las seca y las lija,
finalmente añade un sellador de arcilla micácea
y las cuece al fuego. Su belleza clásica hace
pensar en la prehistórica Haniwa del Japón, que
se compone de figuras situadas alrededor de
túmulos reales. Colección de la Fundación de
Arte Folklórico Internacional en el Museo de
Nuevo México, Santa Fe. Obsequio de
Sallie R. Wagner.

MANUEL VIGIL   48-piece set
    ¾″ to 6¾″ high   1962–1965
Most popular of all Vigil's styles is the Pueblo
Nativity. This set is one of the largest he has
done. Here it is divided into groups forming a
natural progression toward the nucleus of
the Nativity scene. At the end of the procession
are the dancers who take part in the Christmas
celebrations at most New Mexico pueblos:
the Eagle, Deer, and Buffalo Dancers. They are
6½ to 6¾ inches high and incorporate painted
detailing with other materials. The Eagle and
Buffalo Dancers wear leather aprons with
the Avanyu design representing the Plumed
Serpent, emblem of mythic power.
Sallie R. Wagner, Santa Fe, New Mexico.

MANUEL VIGIL   Gruppe von achtundvierzig
    Figuren   1,9 bis 17,1 cm hoch   1962–1965
Der beliebteste der verschiedenen Stile Vigils
ist die Pueblo-Weihnachtskrippe. Die hier
abgebildete Krippe ist eine der größten, die er
produziert hat. Sie wird hier in Gruppen
aufgeteilt, die sich in natürlicher Weise auf den
Mittelpunkt der Szene zubewegen. Am Ende
der Prozession sind die Adler-, Hirsch-, und
Büffeltänzer, die in den meisten Pueblos
von New Mexico an den Weihnachtsfestlich-
keiten teilnehmen. Die Figuren sind 16,5 bis
17,1 cm hoch und ihre detaillierte Bemalung
wird durch die Verwendung anderer
Materialien ergänzt. Die Adler- und Büffeltänzer tragen lederne Schürzen mit dem
Avanyu-Muster, das die gefiederte Schlange,
das Emblem der mythischen Macht, darstellt.
Sallie R. Wagner, Santa Fe, New Mexico.

MANUEL VIGIL   juego de 48 figuras
    de 1.9 cm. a 17.1 cm. de alto   1962–65
Este Nacimiento es uno de los estilos Pueblo
mas populares de Vigil. Este es uno de los más
grandes de sus juegos. Se divide en grupos
que se alinean naturalmente hacia el centro
de la escena del Nacimiento. Al final de la
procesión están los danzarines Aguila, Ciervo,
y Búfalo que participan en las fiestas de Navidad
de casi todos los pueblos indios de Nuevo
México. Estos miden de 16.5 a 17.1 centímetros
de alto y combinan pintura detallada con otros
materiales. Los danzarines Aguila y Búfalo
llevan delantales de cuero decorados con el
bosquejo Avanyu que representa el símbolo de
poder mítico que es la Serpiente Plumada.
Sallie R. Wagner, Santa Fe, Nuevo México.

20

MANUEL VIGIL   48-piece Pueblo-style set
   (*continued*)
Shepherds and other villagers join the
procession to see the Christ Child. Human
figures range from 5¼ to 6¼ inches high.
Detailing on the three shepherds and their
eight sheep is painted on, while the four
villagers wear costumes of cloth and leather
leggings and moccasins and have hair pieces.
The two people at the head of the procession
carry bundles of wood, often presented as a gift
in pueblo Nativities "to warm the Infant in
the stable." In their usual pattern of collaboration, Manuel modeled the figures and Vicenta
did the painting and made the clothes and
accessories.

MANUEL VIGIL   Gruppe von achtundvierzig
   Figuren im Pueblo-Stil   (Fortsetzung)
Hirten und andere Dorfbewohner schließen
sich der Prozession an, um das Christkind
zu schauen. Die Größe der menschlichen
Gestalten variiert von 13,3 bis 15,9 cm Höhe.
Die figürlichen Details der drei Hirten und
ihrer acht Schafe sind gemalt, während die vier
Dorfbewohner Kostüme aus Tuch, lederne
Leggings und Mokassins tragen und echtes
Haar haben. Die zwei Leute an der Spitze der
Prozession tragen Holzbündel, die in
Pueblo-Weihnachtskrippen oft als Geschenk
dargebracht werden, "damit das Christkind im
Stall nicht friert". In ihrer üblichen Zusammen-
arbeit hat Manuel die Gestalten modelliert
und Vicenta sie bemalt und die Kleider und
das Zubehör dafür angefertigt.

MANUEL VIGIL   juego de 48 figuras al
   estilo Pueblo   (*continuación*)
Los pastores y otros aldeanos se juntan en la
procesión para ir a ver al Niño Jesús. Las
figuras miden de 13.3 a 15.9 centímetros de
alto. Hay tres pastores y ocho ovejas con pintura
detallada, mientras cuatro aldeanos llevan
trajes de tela, polainas de cuero, mocasines,
y pelucas. Los dos primeros traen bultos de
lana que muchas veces en los Nacimientos
Pueblo se regalan "para dar calor al Niño Jesús
en el establo." Trabajaron juntos, como siempre,
Manuel modelando las figuras y Vicenta
hiciendo la pintura, la ropa, y los accesorios.

21

MANUEL VIGIL 48-piece Pueblo-style set (*continued*)

Here a little boy urges his horse on to the great event. His war bonnet is more typical of the Plains Indian than the Pueblo, but is the sort of headdress that would appeal to a young boy. He wears a concho belt and squaw boots, with every detail carefully delineated. Four grey donkeys and a cow follow him. The two donkeys in front have real hair glued on for manes and tails, and one carries a bundle of wood. Other than that, all details are painted on with Bisq-stain, a waterproof paint that the Vigils have used in recent years; originally they used tempera.

MANUEL VIGIL Gruppe von achtundvierzig Figuren im Pueblo-Stil (*Fortsetzung*)

Hier spornt ein Junge sein Pferd an, um das große Ereignis schnell zu erreichen. Sein Kriegs-Kopfschmuck typisiert mehr den Prärie- als den Puebloindianer, aber diese Art von Kopfschmuck würde einem Jungen besser gefallen. Er trägt einen *Concho*-Gürtel (einen ledernen Gürtel mit einer Reihe von verzierten "Muscheln" aus Silber) und Frauen-stiefel, worauf jede Einzelheit sorgfältig ausgeführt ist. Vier graue Esel und eine Kuh folgen ihm. Die zwei vorderen Esel haben echtes Haar als Mähnen und Schwänze angeklebt, und einer trägt ein Holzbündel. Sonst sind alle Details mit "Bisq-Farbstoff" angemalt, eine wasserfeste Farbe, welche die Vigils in den letzten Jahren benutzt haben; ursprünglich verwendeten sie Tempera.

MANUEL VIGIL juego de 48 figuras al estilo Pueblo (*continuación*)

Hay aquí un muchachito que anima a su caballo, dirigiéndolo al gran evento. La boina guerrera que lleva es mas típica para los Indios Plains que para los Indios Pueblo, pero es el tipo que le gustaría a un jovencito. Lleva un cinturón concho y botas indias con bosquejos delineados con mucha precisión. Le siguen cuatro burros y una vaca. Para confeccionar las crines y los rabos de los dos burros que van al frente, aplicó crin natural; uno de los burros trae un haz de leña. Durante los últimos años los Vigil vienen utilizando para los demás detalles un tinte impermeable llamado "Bisq." Al principio utilizaban pintura al temple.

MANUEL VIGIL   48-piece Pueblo-style set
(*continued*)
At last the procession reaches the central
figures of the Nativity. Vigil portrays the
Christ Child as a mature man. His hairstyle
with black sideburns, the serape over the
shoulder, long pants, and Indian boots are
identical to those worn by the adult males.
Mary wears the traditional pueblo black manta
with a woven sash. The woven sash is also
worn by the two large angels watching over
the Holy Family. The Three Wise Men bring
strands of beads and a bowl of precious
turquoise stones. The collector refers to the
little boy with the lollipop as "John the
Baptist." The tiny white puppy is ¾ inches
high, the smallest figure in the set.

MANUEL VIGIL   Gruppe von achtundvierzig
Figuren im Pueblo-Stil   (Fortsetzung)
Endlich erreicht die Prozession die zentralen
Figuren der Weihnachtskrippe. Vigil stellt das
Christkind als einen reifen Mann dar. Sein
Haarstil mit schwarzem Backenbart, die als
Mantel gebrauchte Decke über seiner Schulter
(*serape*), die langen Hosen und Indianerstiefel
gleichen denen, die von erwachsenen Männern
getragen werden. Maria trägt den traditionellen
schwarzen Pueblo-Überwurf (*manta*) mit
einer geflochtenen Schärpe. Geflochtene
Schärpen werden auch von den zwei großen
Engeln getragen, die über die Heilige Familie
wachen. Die drei Weisen bringen Perlenschnüre
und eine Schale mit kostbaren Türkissteinen.
Der Sammler bezeichnet den Knaben mit dem
Lutschbonbon als "Johannes der Täufer." Das
winzige weiße Hündlein, 1,9 cm hoch, ist die
kleinste Figur der ganzen Gruppe.

MANUEL VIGIL   juego de 48 figuras al
estilo Pueblo   (*continuación*)
Por fin, la procesión llega a las figuras principales del Nacimiento. Vigil hace una creación
del Niño Jesús como hombre maduro. Es pare-
cido a los hombres adultos, peinado con patillas
negras, el sarape sobre el hombro, con pantalones largos y las botas indias. La Virgen María
lleva el manto tradicional de los indios pueblo
con una faja tejida. Dos ángeles que vigilan a
la Sagrada Familia también llevan la faja tejida.
Los Tres Reyes Magos traen sartas de cuentas
y un cuenco de turquesas. El coleccionista
llama al muchachito con el chupa-chup "San
Juan Bautista." La figura más pequeña en este
juego es el perrito blanco, que mide
1.9 centímetros de alto.

MANUEL VIGIL   Detail from 48-piece
    Pueblo-style set
Nine of Vigil's Pueblo-style angels are included
in this set and are displayed suspended over
the Nativity scene. In some, the clothes are
painted on (center angel), while for others
(top and bottom), Vicenta Vigil makes the black
mantas and white blouses of cloth with actual
white lace petticoats and real leather squaw
boots. The angels range in size from 6 to 7½
inches long.

MANUEL VIGIL   Ausschnitt aus der Gruppe
    von achtundvierzig Figuren im Pueblo-Stil
Neun der Engel in Vigils Pueblo-Stil gehören
zu dieser Gruppe und schweben über der
Weihnachtskrippe. Bei einigen (z.B. dem Engel
in der Mitte) sind die Kleider gemalt; für
andere (oben und unten) verfertigte Vicenta
Vigil die schwarzen Überwürfe (*mantas*) und
weißen Blusen aus Tuch, die Unterröcke aus
weißen Spitzen und die Frauenstiefel aus
echtem Leder. Die Größe der Engel beträgt
15,2 bis 19,1 cm.

MANUEL VIGIL   detalle del juego de 48
    figuras al estilo Pueblo
Suspendidos sobre el Nacimiento hay nueve
ángeles, creados al estilo Pueblo de Vigil que
forman parte de este juego. Algunos, como el
ángel del centro, tienen la ropa pintada, mientras que otros, como los de más arriba o los de
más abajo, Vicenta Vigil hizo mantos negros y
blusas blancas de tela y enaguas verdaderas
de encaje blanco y las botas auténticas de cuero
que llevan las indias. Los ángeles miden de
15.2 a 19.1 centímetros de alto.

MANUEL VIGIL 15-piece set
  3¾″ to 14″ high 1965
Though Vigil also calls this a Pueblo-style set,
it is far different from his usual interpretation.
The pueblo setting is captured, however, down
to the smallest detail — the graveyard, the
horno (oven), the adobe house complete with
clothesline; to the far right is a small cart
loaded with wood and above it, a corral in
which tiny animals are penned. The larger
animals are made of micaceous clay and the
humans of a darker clay. Two of the Wise Men
carry ollas, while the third bears a platter of
shells (shells signify that they have made a
pilgrimage). Materials include cotton, burlap,
fur, hair, and beads. Cristo Rey Church,
Santa Fe, New Mexico.

MANUEL VIGIL Gruppe von fünfzehn
  Figuren 9,5 bis 35,6 cm hoch 1965
Obwohl Vigil auch diese Gruppe zu seinen
Schöpfungen im Pueblo-Stil zählt, unterscheidet
sie sich weitgehend von seinen sonstigen
Darstellungen. Den Pueblo-Hintergrund hat
er aber bis ins kleinste Detail eingefangen —
den Friedhof, den Ofen (*horno*), das Lehmzie-
gelhäuschen mit Wäscheleine; weiter rechts
befindet sich ein kleiner mit Holz beladener
Karren; darüber sieht man einen Korral, in dem
winzige Tiere eingepfercht sind. Die größeren
Tiere sind aus glimmerhaltigem und die
Menschen aus einem dunkleren Ton gebildet.
Zwei der Weisen tragen Wasserkrüge (*ollas*),
während der dritte eine Schale voll Muscheln
trägt. (Die Muscheln bedeuten, daß die Weisen
eine Pilgerfahrt gemacht haben.) Die Stoffe
sind Baumwolle, Sackleinwand, Fell, Haar und
Perlen. Cristo Rey Kirche, Santa Fe,
New Mexico.

MANUEL VIGIL juego de 15 figuras
  de 9.5 cm. a 35.6 cm. de alto 1965
Aunque Vigil considera este juego como uno al
estilo Pueblo, es muy distinto de su estilo
típico. Sin embargo, reproduce la escena
Pueblo hasta el detalle más fino: el cementerio,
el horno, la casa de adobe, a la cual no le falta
ni el detalle de una cuerda para tender la ropa.
Al extremo, a la derecha, se encuentra una
carretilla llena de lana, y más arriba está el
corral que contiene los animalitos. Los animales
más grandes son de arcilla micácea y los
hombres son de arcilla más oscura. Dos de los
Reyes Magos traen ollas, y el tercero porta un
plato de conchas, prueba de que han ido en una
peregrinación. Los materiales que usó incluyen
algodón, arpillera, piel, pelo, y cuentas.
Iglesia de Cristo Rey, Santa Fe, Nuevo México.

cochiti pueblo

HELEN CORDERO is the most famous representative of her pueblo and holds a unique position in Southwest pottery arts. When she originated the Storyteller figure in 1964, she raised the status of figurative works in clay from a curiosity to an art form. Her Storyteller is a large seated figure ranging from seven to twenty inches high, with from three to thirty children clambering over it and, occasionally, a puppy. It was inspired, she says, by her grandfather, Santiago Quintana. "He was known by everybody as a really good storyteller. All of us grandchildren would crowd around him to listen." The theme has its roots in Indian tradition, too, where one member of a tribe, usually a chief or grandparent who had a gift for storytelling, would pass on the history and legends of the tribe to the children. Her Storytellers captivated the public immediately and took major awards.

Through the years she has developed many new themes. The Drummer, a seated male figure playing a drum, was inspired by her husband, Fred Cordero, one of Cochiti's finest drum makers. Others are Singing Mother, The Water Carrier, Pueblo Father, Night Crier, and The Children's Hour, a variation on her Storyteller. One of her newest themes is a turtle with children riding piggyback on it.

She made her first Nativity scene in

HELEN CORDERO ist die berühmteste Vertreterin ihres Pueblos und genießt in der südwestindianischen Töpferkunst eine einzigartige Stellung. Als sie 1964 die 'Erzählerfigur' erfand, erhöhte sie den Rang der Tonfiguren von einer Kuriosität zu einer Kunstform. Ihre Erzähler sind große, sitzende, von 17,8 bis 50,8 cm hohe Gestalten, mit drei bis dreißig auf ihnen herumkletternden Kindern – und gelegentlich einem jungen Hund. Sie erklärt, sie sei von ihrem Großvater Santiago Quintana inspiriert worden, die Erzählerfiguren zu schaffen: "Von allen Leuten wurde er als hervorragender Erzähler anerkannt. Jedes von uns Enkelkindern drängte sich um ihn, um ihm zuzuhören." Das Thema wurzelt auch in der indianischen Tradition, wonach ein Stammesmitglied, gewöhnlich ein Häuptling oder Großvater, der gut erzählen konnte, die Geschichte und Legenden des Stammes an die Kinder weitergab. Ihre Erzählerfiguren haben das Publikum sofort bezaubert und wichtige Preise erworben.

Im Laufe der Jahre hat sie viele neue Themen entwickelt. Der Trommler, eine sitzende, trommelspielende Männerfigur, entstand unter dem Einfluß ihres Ehemannes Fred Cordero, eines der besten Trommelhersteller Cochitis. Weitere Themen sind "Singende Mutter", "Der Wasserträger", "Pueblo Vater", "Nacht-Ausrufer" und "Die Kinderstunde", die eine Variation ihres "Erzählers" ist. Eines ihrer neuesten Themen ist eine Schildkröte, auf deren Rücken Kinder reiten.

Sie schuf ihre erste Weihnachtskrippe

HELEN CORDERO es la representante más famosa de Cochiti y ocupa una posición especial en el arte de la cerámica del Suroeste. En 1964, cuando se originó la figura del Narrador de Cuentos, elevó la reputación de las obras figurativas de arcilla desde una curiosidad hasta una forma de arte. Su Narrador de Cuentos es una figura grande, sentada, que mide de 17.8 a 50.8 centímetros de alto con niños (de tres a treinta en total) que suben gateando sobre ella y, a veces, un perrito. Dice que su Narrador se inspiró de su abuelo, Santiago Quintana. "Todos le consideraban un narrador de cuentos de primer orden. Todos nosotros (sus nietos) nos congregábamos alrededor de él para escucharle." El tema también tiene sus orígenes en la tradición de los indios: un miembro de la tribu, generalmente un jefe o abuelo dotado con la capacidad de narrar cuentos, transmitía la historia y las leyendas de la tribu a los niños. Los Narradores de Cuentos de Helen encantaron al público inmediatamente y ganaron premios importantes.

A través de los años Helen ha desarrollado muchos temas nuevos. El Tamborilero, un hombre sentado y tocando el tambor, se inspiró de su marido Fred Cordero, quien es un fabricante excelente de tambores en Cochiti. Otras de sus figuras son La Madre Cantando, El Aguatero, el Padre del Pueblo, El Pregonero del Pueblo, y La Hora Infantil, que es una variación de su Narrador de Cuentos. Una tortuga que lleva niños a cuestas es uno de sus temas más recientes.

Helen hizó su primer Nacimiento en

HELEN CORDERO   16-piece set
   1½″ to 6½″ high   1972
The artist's husband made this stable of cotton-wood. He also made the hunter's bow and the cradle lined with fleece. Helen notes: "That's the kind of cradleboard we always put our babies in the first day they are born." (See detail in frontispiece.) Of the man with the sack over his shoulder (far right fore-ground), she says, "He's carrying costumes that the boys use for dancing; the Indians knew Jesus would need what the boys use. The little boy with his hands over his head (center) is saying, 'Oh, what a beautiful baby!'" This scene is on a Museum of New Mexico Christmas card. International Folk Art Foundation Collection in the Museum of New Mexico, Santa Fe.

HELEN CORDERO   Gruppe von sechzehn
   Figuren 3,8 bis 16,5 cm hoch   1972
Der Gatte der Künstlerin fertigte diesen Stall aus Cottonwood (einer Pappelart). Er machte auch den Bogen des Jägers und die mit Fell gefütterte Wiege. Helen bemerkt: "Das ist die Wiegenart ("cradleboard"), in die wir immer unsere Babys schon am Tage der Geburt legen." (Siehe Detailausschnitt im Titelbild.) In bezug auf den Mann mit dem Sack auf der Schulter (vorne weit rechts), sagt sie: "Er bringt Kostüme, die die Jungen für Tänze benutzen; die Indianer wuβten, daβ Jesus das benötigen würde, was die Jungen gebrauchen. Der kleine Junge mit den Händen über seinem Kopf (Mitte) sagt: 'Ach, was für ein schönes Baby!'." Diese Szene erscheint auf einer Weihnachtskarte des Museums von New Mexico. Sammlung der Internationalen Volkskunst-Stiftung im Museum von New Mexico, Santa Fe.

HELEN CORDERO   juego de 16 piezas
   de 3.8 cm. a 16.5 cm. de alto   1972
El marido de la artista creó este establo en madera de álamo. También hizo el arco de cazador y la cuna forrada de lana. Helen observa: "Ese es el tipo de cuna portátil en que siempre ponemos a los niños el día que nacen." (Nótese el detalle en el frontispicio.) Del hombre que trae el saco sobre el hombro (a la derecha extrema en el primer plano) dice: "Trae trajes que usan los muchachos cuando bailan; los indios sabían que el Niño Jesús necesitaría lo que emplean los muchachos. El niño que levanta las manos sobre la cabeza dice: 'Ah, ¡que niño bonito!'" Esta escena está en una tarjeta de Navidad del Museo de Nuevo México. La Colección de Arte Folklórico Internacional del Museo de Nuevo México, Santa Fe.

HELEN CORDERO   17-piece set
   1½″ to 6½″ high   1972
The addition of children and puppies to the
Nativity scene is a Helen Cordero trademark.
Also, her cattle always bear the Cochiti brand
(visible here on the donkey), and, as in her
other themes, the people always have their eyes
closed and mouths open. "They do much
praying and thinking." The tiny ears of corn
on the heads of the two women are removable;
one of the women carries a bowl of bread in her
hands. Helen notes: "All of the ladies of
Cochiti take to the Infant Jesus whatever we
have on Christmas morning." This set was
featured in the book, *Art and Indian
Individualists*, 1975. Katherine H. Rust
Children's Collection, Albuquerque,
New Mexico.

HELEN CORDERO   Gruppe mit siebzehn
Figuren   3,8 bis 16,5 cm hoch   1972
Die Bereicherung der Weihnachtskrippe mit
Kindern und Hündlein ist ein Markenzeichen
Helen Corderos. Ihr Ton-Vieh trägt immer
das Brandmal von Cochiti (hier auf dem Esel
sichtbar), und wie in ihren anderen Darstellungen halten die Menschen immer die Augen
geschlossen und den Mund geöffnet. "Sie beten
und denken viel." Die winzigen Getreideähren
auf den Köpfen der beiden Frauen sind
abnehmbar; eine der Frauen trägt in den
Händen eine Schüssel mit Brot. Helen bemerkt:
"Alle Damen von Cochiti bringen dem
Christkind das, was wir am Weihnachtsmorgen
essen." Diese Gruppe wurde in dem Buch
Kunst und indianische Individualisten
(*Art and Indian Individualists*, 1975)
abgebildet. Katherine H. Rust Kinderkunstsammlung, Albuquerque, New Mexico.

HELEN CORDERO   juego de 17 piezas
   de 3.8 cm. a 16.5 cm. de alto   1972
Una característica única de Helen Cordero es
que ella incluye niños y perritos en el Nacimiento. También, su ganado siempre lleva la
marca de Cochiti que se ve aquí en el burro, y,
como en sus otros temas, la gente siempre tiene
los ojos cerrados y la boca abierta. "Pasan
mucho tiempo rezando y meditando." Las
pequeñas mazorcas de maíz se pueden quitar
de la cabeza de las dos mujeres; una mujer
trae una vasija de pan en las manos. Helen
observa: "En la mañana de Navidad, cada
mujer de Cochiti le trae al Niño Jesús lo que
tenemos." Esta juego apareció en el libro,
Arte e Indios Individualistas, 1975. Colección
Infantil de Katherine H. Rust, Albuquerque,
Nuevo México.

28

1970. That year the Heard Museum of Phoenix, which already had many of her pieces in its permanent collection, asked her to do something different. She recalls, "I thought of doing Noah's Ark. Then I thought of the Nativity, how we come to greet the Infant Jesus in our church, and I thought, 'I'll do it our way — the Indian way.'" She entered the set in the Heard's Annual Indian Arts and Crafts Exhibit, where it won the Best of Show award. That December it was featured in the museum's folk art exhibit and has been exhibited every Christmas since. In 1974 the noted folk art collector, Alexander Girard, commissioned her to do a 250-piece Nativity scene. "He sketched every piece he wanted, down to the smallest figures — birds, owls, cats." It is now in the Girard Foundation Collection at the Museum of International Folk Art in Santa Fe. This museum has commissioned her to do a number of sets over the years and exhibits them each Christmas. Helen's Nativities are always called "Christmas Morning in Cochiti." She says, "I try to show everything the way we do it in Cochiti — the clothes we wear, the gifts we bring, and our animals here. I never use sheep in my Nativities because we don't have them in Cochiti."

Helen was born in Cochiti on June 17,

im Jahre 1970. Das Heard Museum in Phoenix, das schon viele ihrer Objekte in seiner ständigen Sammlung besaß, bat sie damals, etwas Neues zu machen. Sie erinnert sich: "Zuerst dachte ich daran, die Arche Noahs zu gestalten; dann dachte ich an die Weihnachtskrippe und wie wir zusammenkommen, das Christkind in unserer Kirche zu grüßen, und ich habe mich entschlossen: 'Ich werde sie auf unsere Weise — auf die indianische Weise — gestalten.'" Sie zeigte die Gruppe in der jährlichen Ausstellung Indianischer Kunsthandwerker des Heard Museums und erhielt dafür den ersten Preis. Im Dezember desselben Jahres wurde die Gruppe in der Volkskunstausstellung des Heard Museums ausgestellt und seitdem ist sie dort jedes Jahr zu Weihnachten zu sehen. 1974 beauftragte sie der bekannte Volkskunstsammler Alexander Girard, eine Weihnachtskrippe mit 250 Figuren herzustellen. "Jede einzelne Figur hat er skizziert, einschließlich der kleinen Figuren wie Vögel, Eulen und Katzen." Sie steht jetzt in der Sammlung der Girard-Stiftung im Museum für Internationale Volkskunst in Santa Fe. Dieses Museum hat sie im Lauf der Jahre beauftragt, mehrere Gruppen anzufertigen, und stellt diese jedes Jahr während der Weihnachtszeit aus. Die Weihnachtskrippen Helens heißen immer "Weihnachtsmorgen in Cochiti". "Ich versuche, alles so zu zeigen, wie wir es in Cochiti machen," erklärt sie, "— unsere Kleidung, die Geschenke, die wir bringen, und unsere hiesigen Tiere. Ich gestalte niemals Schafe für meine Weihnachtskrippen, da wir in Cochiti keine besitzen."

Helen wurde am 17. Juni 1915 in

1970. Ese mismo año el Museo Heard de Phoenix, que ya tenía muchas piezas de ella en la colección permanente, le pidió que hiciera algo diferente. Ella recuerda: "Pensé en hacer el Arca de Noé. Entonces, pensé en el Nacimiento, en que venimos a la iglesia para saludar al Niño Jesús, y me dije, 'Lo haré en nuestro estilo — el estilo indio.'" Presentó el juego en la exhibición Anual Heard de las Artes y Artesanías Indios y ganó el Premio al Mejor de la exhibición. En diciembre del mismo año y en Navidad, cada año, lo exhiben en la exposición de arte del pueblo en el museo. En 1974 el famoso coleccionista de arte del pueblo, Alexander Girard, le encargó que creara un Nacimiento de 250 piezas. "Esbozó cada pieza que quería, aún las figuras menores: pájaros, lechuzas, y gatos." Ahora está en la Colección de la Asociación Girard en el Museo de Arte Folklórico Internacional de Santa Fe. Este museo le encargó que hiciera varios juegos sobre los años, y los exhibe anualmente en la Navidad. Los Nacimientos de Helen siempre se llaman "Mañana de Navidad en Cochiti." Dice: "Trato de presentar todo como lo hacemos en Cochiti — la ropa que llevamos, los regalos que traemos, y nuestros animales de aquí. Nunca incluyo ovejas en mis Nacimientos porque no las hay en Cochiti."

Helen nació el 17 de julio de 1915, en

1915, and has lived there all of her life. She attended Saint Catherine's School in Santa Fe from the third through the eighth grade. A devout Catholic, she carries a small statue of Saint Anthony of Padua in her purse "wherever I go. He is so special to me." Since he is always shown carrying a child (the Christ Child), he seems a fitting companion for her and bears a close kinship to her creations. She and her husband had four children and adopted two sons; they now have eleven grandchildren. Considering her present international reputation as a ceramist, it is surprising that she did not start working in clay until she was forty years old. As she says, "Everyone around me was making beautiful things, and I wanted to do something, too." Under the tutelage of a friend, she tried making pots, but "they just didn't turn out right." Her friend then suggested she try figures. Helen did. "Suddenly it was just like a flower blooming. I knew that it is what I was meant to do."

Cochiti geboren und hat ihr ganzes Leben dort verbracht. Sie ging in die Grundschule der Heiligen Katharina in Santa Fe von der dritten bis zur achten Klasse. Sie ist eine sehr fromme Katholikin und trägt ein kleines Bildnis des Heiligen Antonio von Padua in der Geldtasche: "Wo ich auch hingehe — er ist für mich etwas ganz Besonderes." Da er in Darstellungen immer das Christkind trägt, scheint er ihr ein geeigneter Begleiter zu sein, und ihre Schöpfungen spiegeln eine innere Verwandtschaft mit ihm wider. Sie und ihr Mann hatten vier Kinder und zwei adoptierte Söhne; jetzt haben sie auch elf Enkelkinder. Zieht man ihren gegenwärtigen internationalen Ruf als Keramikerin in Betracht, so ist man erstaunt, daß sie erst im Alter von 40 Jahren begonnen hat, Ton zu bearbeiten. Sie sagt einfach: "Die Menschen, die um mich waren, schufen schöne Gegenstände, und ich wollte auch etwas machen." Unter der Anleitung einer Freundin hat sie versucht, Töpfe zu machen, aber "sie fielen immer schlecht aus." Ihre Freundin schlug ihr dann vor, sie sollte versuchen, Figuren zu gestalten. Das tat sie. "Plötzlich war es, als blühte eine Blume. Ich wußte, daß die Vorsehung es mir so bestimmt hatte."

Cochiti, donde ha pasado toda su vida. Asistió a la Escuela Santa Catalina en Santa Fe del tercero al octavo año. Como devota Católica, trae en su bolsa, "a cualquier lugar que va," una estatuita pequeña de San Antonio de Padua. "Significa tanto para mí." Como siempre aparece trayendo un niño (el Niño Jesús), parece ser un compañero apropriado para ella y se identifica mucho con sus creaciones. Ella y su esposo tuvieron cuatro hijos y adoptaron dos más; ahora tienen once nietos. En vista de su fama internacional como ceramista, es sorprendente que no comenzara trabajando en cerámica hasta que tuviera cuarenta años. Como dice ella: "Todos alrededor a mi creaban cosas bellas, y yo quería hacer algo, también." Bajo la tutela de un amigo, trató de hacer ollas, pero "no resultaron como debían." Su amigo entonces sugirió que hiciera figuras. Helena así lo hizo. "En seguida fue como una flor abriéndose. Supe entonces qué era lo que debía hacer."

ADA SUINA started making pottery only three years ago and made her first Nativity set just over two years ago. "I began with little bowls and figures and then I did larger things." Her Storyteller and Drummer figures are about ten inches high. These and her Nativities have already brought her recognition. The new Museum of Albuquerque, which opened in May, 1979, purchased one of her Nativity sets and a Drummer for its permanent collection and has one of her Storytellers on loan.

"I have made a few bowls, but I do mostly figures now. Sometimes when I have clay left over from my figures, I use it for making little bowls and miniature birds, turtles, and owls. I do everything the old way and that is hard. We travel over bumpy roads to get our different clays." A unique feature of her recent work is the addition of a third color to the traditional Cochiti red and black. This is a pale orange slip made of a special clay that is light yellow before firing. "I think firing is the hardest part. My mother-in-law, Aurelia Suina, taught me how to fire, and we still sometimes work together. My cousin, Virginia Naranjo, first taught me

ADA SUINA begann erst vor drei Jahren, Töpferwaren anzufertigen und gestaltete vor zwei Jahren ihre erste Weihnachtskrippe. "Ich fing mit Schüsselchen und Figuren an, und dann stellt ich größere Sachen her." Sowohl ihre Erzähler- und Trommlerfiguren, die etwa 25 cm hoch sind, als auch ihre Weihnachtskrippen haben ihr schon Anerkennung gebracht. Das neue Museum von Albuquerque, das im Mai 1979 eröffnet wurde, kaufte eine ihrer Weihnachtskrippen und einen Trommler für seine Dauerausstellung und besitzt einen ihrer Erzähler als Leihgabe.

"Ich habe einige Schüsseln geschaffen, aber jetzt mache ich hauptsächlich Figuren. Manchmal, wenn nach Gestaltung der Figuren etwas Ton übrigbleibt, verwende ich ihn für die Anfertigung kleiner Schüsseln und Miniaturvögel, -schildkröten und -eulen. Ich mache alles auf die alte Weise, und das ist schwer. Wir reisen über unebene Straßen, um unsere verschiedenen Tonarten zu holen." Ein einzigartiges Merkmal ihrer neueren Töpferarbeiten ist die Verwendung einer dritten Farbe neben dem traditionellen Cochiti-Rot und -Schwarz. Es ist eine blaß orange Farbe, die beim Brennen aus einem besonderen hellgelben, geschlämmten Tonüberzug entsteht. "Das Brennen ist meiner Meinung nach die schwierigste Phase. Meine Schwiegermutter Aurelia Suina hat mir das Brennen beigebracht, und manchmal arbeiten wir noch zusammen. Meine Cousine Virginia Naranjo war die erste,

ADA SUINA comenzó a crear cerámica hace solamente tres años. Hace dos años que hizo su primer Nacimiento. "Comencé con escudillas y figuras y luego hice objetos más grandes." Sus figuras de Narradores de Cuentos y del Tamborilero miden como 25 centímetros de alto. Ada ha llamado la atención por estas figuras así como también por sus Nacimientos. El nuevo Museo de Albuquerque, que abierto en mayo de 1979, compró un juego de Ada y uno de sus Tamborileros para exhibirlos en su colección permanente. También han conseguido prestado uno de sus Narradores de Cuentos.

"Hice unas pocas vasijas en el pasado, pero ahora hago mayormente figuras. A veces, cuando me queda un poco de arcilla de las figuras, la uso para crear vasijas pequeñas y pájaros, tortugas, y lechuzas en miniatura. Siempre trabajo empleando métodos antiguos, lo cuál es muy difícil. Viajamos por carreteras llenas de baches para conseguir los diferentes tipos de arcilla." Una característica única de su obra es que agrega un tercer color al rojo y negro ya tradicional en Cochiti. Es un sellador de color naranja pálida que resulta de un tipo de arcilla especial que tiene el color amarillo antes de cocerla. "Creo que el cocido al fuego es la parte más difícil. Mi suegra, Aurelia Suina, me lo enseñó y todavía trabajamos juntas a veces. El arte de la cerámica me lo enseñó mi

ADA SUINA   12-piece set
  2″ to 5″ high   1976
When the artist saw this photograph, she said,
"That is the first or second Nativity set I ever
made. I do much better now!" Her recent work
is more refined, but this has a special charm,
nevertheless. Pointing to the Three Wise Men
bearing their gifts of rabbits, corn, and a bowl,
she notes, "We were taught that the Wise Men
brought the necessities, not fancy gifts."
She includes an angel with a black border
design on its wings and a shepherd with two
sheep and two cows. The Baby Jesus and the
metate-style cradle are two separate pieces,
though counted as one. Museum of Northern
Arizona Shop, Flagstaff, Arizona.

ADA SUINA   Gruppe von zwölf Figuren
  5,1 bis 12,7 cm hoch   1976
Als die Künstlerin dieses Foto anschaute,
sagte sie: "Das ist die erste oder zweite
Weihnachtskrippe, die ich je geschaffen habe.
Jetzt mache ich sie viel besser!" Ihre neueren
Arbeiten sind verfeinert, aber diese
Weihnachtskrippe hat trotzdem einen
besonderen Reiz. Ada deutete auf die drei
Weisen, die Hasen, Mais und eine Schale als
Geschenke bringen, mit der Bemerkung:
"Man lehrte uns, daβ die Weisen unentbehrliche
Gegenstände brachten, nicht Luxusgeschenke".
Sie fügt diesen Gestalten einen Engel mit einem
schwarzen Randmuster auf den Flügeln und
einen Hirten mit zwei Schafen und zwei
Kühen hinzu. Das Christkind und die Wiege im
Metate-Stil sind zwei einzelne Stücke, obwohl
sie als eins gezählt werden. Verkaufsstelle des
Museums von Northern Arizona,
Flagstaff, Arizona.

ADA SUINA   juego de 12 figuras
  de 5.1 cm. a 12.7 cm. de alto   1976
Cuando la artista vio la fotografía, dijo: "Este
es el primero o segundo Nacimiento que hice.
¡Ahora trabajo mucho mejor!" Su obra reciente
es más refinada, pero ésta tiene un encanto
especial, sin embargo. Señalando a los Tres
Reyes Magos trayendo regalos — conejos, maíz,
y una vasija — nos dice: "Se nos ha enseñado
que los Reyes Magos trajeron los necesidades y
no regalos de lujo." Incluye un ángel que
tiene un dibujo negro en el borde de las alas y
un pastor con dos ovejas y dos vacas. El Niño
Jesús y la cuna al estilo metate consiste en dos
piezas distintas, aunque se consideran una
sola. Tienda del Museo del Norte de Arizona,
Flagstaff, Arizona.

pottery making." Virginia is the daughter-in-law of Frances Naranjo Suina, also noted for Nativity scenes.

Ada was born in Cochiti on May 30, 1930, the daughter of Eluterio and Bernina Cordero. Her mother did not make pottery, but Ada received inspiration from her grandmother, Stephanita Herrera. "Her work is in museums; all of it is signed with her initials, S.A.H. She did great big pots — dough pots, we call them — and pitchers with lizard-head spouts." Ada's father made drums and taught this popular Cochiti craft to her husband, Tony. Tony also collaborates with Ada, making mangers of cedar wood for her Nativities, and two of their daughters are making figures in clay now. Ada observes that she has not been able to devote as much time to her craft as she would like because of raising their eleven children. "Now that my youngest is in school, I hope to have more time for my pottery."

die mir Unterricht im Töpfern erteilte." Virginia ist die Schwiegertochter von Frances Naranjo Suina, die ebenfalls für ihre Weihnachtskrippen bekannt ist.

Ada wurde am 30. Mai 1930 als Tochter von Eluterio und Bernina Cordero in Cochiti geboren. Ihre Mutter war keine Töpferin, aber ihre Groß-mutter Stephanita Herrera hat sie für die Töpferkunst begeistert. "Ihre Tonwaren, alle mit den Anfangsbuchstaben ihres Namens, S.A.H., signiert, stehen in den Museen. Sie fertigte große Gefäße — Teigtöpfe nennen wir sie — und Krüge mit eidechsenkopfförmigen Ausgüssen." Adas Vater stellte Trommeln her und brachte ihrem Ehemann Tony dieses beliebte Cochiti-Kunsthandwerk bei. Tony arbeitet auch mit Ada zusammen, indem er Krippen aus Zedernholz für ihre Weihnachtsszenen schnitzt, und zwei ihrer Töchter modellieren jetzt Tonfiguren. Ada bemerkt, daß sie wegen der Erziehung ihrer elf Kinder der Töpferkunst nicht so viel Zeit widmen konnte, wie sie es gerne getan hätte. "Da mein Jüngstes jetzt in die Schule geht, hoffe ich, meiner Keramik mehr Zeit widmen zu können."

prima, Virginia Naranjo. Virginia es la nuera de Frances Naranjo Suina, artista bien conocida por sus Nacimientos.

Ada, hija de Eluterio y Bernina Cordero, nació el 30 de mayo en 1930. Su madre no era ceramista, pero Ada se inspiró en su abuela, Stephanita Herrera. "Su obra se exhibe en museos; cada objeto está firmado con las iniciales de su nombre, S.A.H. Creó ollas enormas, que llamamos ollas de pasta, y cántaros con los picos en forma de cabezas de lagarto." El padre de Ada construía tambores y le enseñó este arte popular de Cochiti a su marido, Toni. Toni también colabora con Ada, haciendo cunas de cedro para sus Nacimientos. Dos hijas suyas han empezado a crear figuras de arcilla. Ada observa que la educación de los once hijos no le ha permitido dedicarse como quisiera a su arte. "Ahora, que mi hijo menor está en la escuela, espero tener más tiempo para la cerámica."

FRANCES NARANJO SUINA has been making pottery for over fifty years. In the special pottery issue of *Arizona Highways*, May 1974, she was called "one of the skilled bowl and pot makers of Cochiti Pueblo." At the age of twenty-five when she began, she did functional pieces such as bean pots and sugar bowls and, once, a six-piece place setting of dinnerware. In recent years she has become noted for her clay figures, and about ten years ago she began making Nativity sets. In 1975 one of her sets was featured in the Museum of Northern Arizona exhibition, *Nacimientos: Manger Scenes from the Sallie Wagner Collection*. "In the last few years," she says, "I have been getting more orders for my Nativities, but in 1978 it seemed I had orders for nothing but angels." She does angels in various sizes, some as high as seven inches, and her miniatures have also been in great demand. "I put little holes in their wings because many people hang them on their Christmas trees." Recently her clay pigs in miniatures and larger sizes have become popular. She notes: "I started with small figures, but now I am making some Storytellers that are fifteen inches high." These took First Prizes at both the 1973 and 1974 Indian Market in Santa Fe. She has not

FRANCES NARANJO SUINA stellt schon seit über fünfzig Jahren Töpferwaren her. In der Sondernummer der Zeitschrift *Arizona Highways* über indianische Töpferkunst (Mai 1974) nannte man sie "eine der erfahrenen Töpferinnen von Cochiti Pueblo". Als sie mit fünfundzwanzig Jahren anfing, stellte sie Gebrauchsgegenstände wie Bohnentöpfe und Zuckerdosen her, und einmal hat sie ein Tafelgeschirr für sechs Personen angefertigt. Neuerdings ist sie durch ihre Tonfiguren bekannt geworden, und vor etwa zehn Jahren hat sie angefangen, Weihnachtskrippen zu produzieren. Im Jahre 1975 wurde eine ihrer Gruppen in einer Ausstellung des Museums von Northern Arizona unter dem Titel "Nacimientos: Weihnachtskrippen aus der Sallie Wagner-Sammlung" zur Schau gestellt. "In den letzten Jahren," sagt sie, "habe ich mehr Bestellungen für meine Weihnachtskrippen erhalten, aber im Jahre 1978 schien es, als würden nur Weihnachtsengel bestellt." Sie fertigt Engel in verschiedenen Größen an — einige beinahe 18 cm hoch — aber auch ihre Miniaturen sind sehr begehrt. "Ich mache kleine Löcher in ihre Flügel, weil viele Leute ihren Weihnachtsbaum damit schmücken." Neuerdings sind ihre Tonschweine, Miniaturen sowohl als auch größere Formen, populär geworden. Sie bemerkt: "Ich fing mit kleinen Figuren an, aber jetzt mache ich einige Erzähler, die 38,1 cm hoch sind." Diese Erzähler haben 1973 und 1974 im Santa Fe-Indianermarkt den ersten Preis gewonnen. In letzter Zeit hat sie

FRANCES NARANJO SUINA ha estado haciendo cerámica por más de cincuenta años. En el número especial sobre cerámica de la revista *Arizona Highways*, mayo de 1974, fue llamada "una de las más hábiles ceramistas de vasijas y ollas del pueblo Cochiti." Cuando comenzó a la edad de veinticinco años, realizaba piezas de función utilitaria como ollas para frijoles, azucareras, y, en una ocasión, hizo un juego de vajilla de seis piezas. En los últimos años se ha hecho conocer por sus figuras de arcilla y aproximadamente hace diez años comenzó a hacer Nacimientos. En 1975 uno de sus juegos se presentó en la exhibición del Museo del Norte de Arizona, *Nacimientos: Escenas de Pesebres de la Colección de Sallie Wagner*. "En los últimos años," ella dice, "he recibido más pedidos de mis Nacimientos, pero en 1978 parece que sólo recibí pedidos de ángeles." Frances crea ángeles de varios tamaños, algunos de hasta 18 centímetros de alto, y hay una gran demanda por sus obras en miniatura. "Pongo pequeños agujeros en las alas de los ángeles porque muchas personas los cuelgan en el árbol de Navidad." Recientemente sus puercos de arcilla en miniatura y de tamaños más grandes se han popularizado. Frances señala: "Comencé con pequeñas figuras pero ahora me encuentro haciendo Narradores de Cuentos que tienen hasta 38.1 centímetros de alto." Estos recibieron el primer premio en el Mercado Indio de Santa Fe, en

FRANCES SUINA   4-piece set
1¾″ to 3¼″ high   ca. 1972
In this amusing interpretation, Joseph and Mary
seem rather alarmed, while the cow merely
looks curious. The artist notes: "That was one
of the first Nativities I did. In the sets I do
now I make a clay cradle shaped like a bowl;
the Baby may be separate or in one piece with
the cradle. Sometimes I do a set with just
four figures, but mostly I do larger sets with
eleven figures, some six inches high. In those
there are Saint Joseph, the Blessed Mother, the
Baby, the Three Kings, an angel, a burro, a
lamb, cow, and camel. All my people wear
traditional Cochiti clothes." Sallie R. Wagner,
Santa Fe, New Mexico.

FRANCES SUINA   Gruppe von vier Figuren
4,4 bis 8,3 cm hoch   ca. 1972
In dieser amüsanten Darstellung scheinen
Joseph und Maria ziemlich beängstigt zu sein,
während die Kuh nur neugierig ausschaut.
Die Künstlerin bemerkt: "Das war eine der
ersten Weihnachtskrippen, die ich gemacht
habe. In den Gruppen, die ich heute mache,
gestalte ich eine schüsselförmige Wiege aus
Ton; das Christkind wird entweder separat
gestaltet oder zusammen mit der Wiege in
einem Stück. Manchmal gestalte ich eine
Gruppe mit nur vier Figuren, aber meistens
verfertige ich größere Gruppen mit elf Figuren,
die bis 15 cm hoch sind. Zu diesen Gruppen
gehören der Heilige Joseph, die Heilige
Jungfrau, das Christkind, die drei Könige, ein
Engel, ein Esel, ein Schaf, eine Kuh und ein
Kamel. Meine Leute tragen alle die
traditionelle Cochiti Tracht." Sallie R. Wagner,
Santa Fe, New Mexico.

FRANCES SUINA   juego de cuatro piezas
de 4.4 cm. a 8.3 cm. de alto   circa 1972
En esta divertida interpretación, José y María
parecen alarmados mientras la vaca simplemente mira con curiosidad. La artista señala:
"Ese fue uno de los primeros Nacimientos que
hice. En los de ahora hago una cuna de arcilla
en forma de vasija; el Niño Jesús puede estar
separado o en una pieza con la cuna. A veces
hago un juego con cuatro figuras pero en
general los hago mayores con 11 figuras algunas
de 15 centímetros de alto. En éstas se encuentran San José, la Madre Bendita, el Niño Jesús,
los Tres Reyes Magos, un ángel, un burro, un
cordero, una vaca, y un camello. Todos mis
personajes llevan ropas tradicionales de
Cochiti." Sallie R. Wagner, Santa Fe, Nuevo
México.

entered anything lately because, as she says, "All of my pieces have sold the minute they are fired."

Frances was born on September 2, 1902, at San Ildefonso Pueblo, the youngest of the five daughters of Juan Roybal. When she was less than a year old, both parents died, and she was taken into Saint Catherine's Orphanage at Santa Fe. When one of her sisters married a Cochiti man, she brought Frances to Cochiti to attend school there. Later Frances returned to Saint Catherine's to finish her schooling. Her first husband was named Naranjo; following his death, she married Suina. One of her six children, Louis Naranjo, lives nearby and helps her with her firing. She uses the local clays and, unlike most modern potters, does not use commercial brushes for detailing but makes her own in the old way from the yucca plant.

nicht mehr an Wettbewerben teilgenommen, weil "sich alle meine Töpferwaren gleich nach dem Brennen sofort verkaufen."

Frances wurde am 2. September 1902 als jüngste von den fünf Töchtern Juan Roybals in San Ildefonso geboren. Ehe sie ein Jahr alt war, starben beide Eltern, und sie wurde im Waisenhaus der Heiligen Katharina in Santa Fe aufgenommen. Als eine ihrer Schwestern einen Mann aus Cochiti heiratete, brachte sie Frances dorthin, so daß sie in die dortige Schule gehen konnte. Später kehrte sie in die Schule der Heiligen Katharina zurück, um ihre Schulausbildung abzuschließen. Ihr erster Mann hieß Naranjo; nach seinem Tode heiratete sie Suina. Eines ihrer sechs Kinder, Louis Naranjo, wohnt in der Nähe und hilft ihr beim Brennen ihrer Töpferwaren. Sie gebraucht die örtlichen Tone, und im Gegensatz zu den meisten modernen Töpfern benutzt sie keine gekauften Pinsel für die Bemalung, sondern fertigt auf alte Weise ihre eigenen aus der Yucca-Pflanze an.

1973 y 1974. No ha participado en ninguna exhibición últimamente porque, como ella misma dice, "Todas mis piezas se venden inmediatamente que las acabo."

Frances nació el 2 de septiembre de 1902, en el pueblo de San Ildefonso, y es la menor de cinco hijas de Juan Roybal. Cuando tenía menos de un año, sus padres fallecieron y la pusieron en el orfanato de Santa Catarina, en Santa Fe. Cuando una de sus hermanas se casó con un hombre de Cochiti, se llevó a Frances para vivir en Cochiti y asistir a la escuela. Más tarde, Frances volvió a Santa Catarina para terminar la escuela. Su primer esposo se llamaba Naranjo; cuando enviudó, se casó con Suina. Uno de sus seis hijos, Luis Naranjo, vive cerca de ella y la ayuda con el cocimiento de su cerámica. Emplea la arcilla del lugar y, a diferencia de la mayoría de los ceramistas modernos, para colocar los detalles no usa pinceles comerciales sino que los hace ella misma con la planta de la yuca como en los tiempos pasados.

DOROTHY TRUJILLO is the oldest of six sisters, all of whom are potters and make Nacimientos. She notes, "I began making Nativities about ten years ago. After a time I stopped, but then seven years ago I started making them again." She has been working with clay ever since she can remember. Born in Jemez Pueblo on April 26, 1932, she is the daughter of Louis Loretto, a native of Jemez, and Carrie Reid of Laguna Pueblo. She attended San Diego Mission School and spent school vacations helping her mother and grandmother with their pottery. "The first things I did on my own, at age ten, were small figures — women holding one or two babies, and then figures in canoes; I would name each figure, such as 'Sitting Bull.' Later I did bowls and wedding vases."

When she married Onofre Trujillo and moved to Cochiti, she was no longer allowed to use Jemez clay, as each pueblo reserves its clay for use within the pueblo. Eventually she was given the right to use Cochiti clays and learned to work with them by helping Onofre's aunt, Damacia Cordero. "First I made pottery just like hers, but she told me I should start making it in my own way and I did." Following the tradition of her mother's people, she made Laguna-style pots and water jars. "Then

DOROTHY TRUJILLO ist die älteste von sechs Schwestern, die alle Töpferinnen sind und *Nacimientos* anfertigen. Sie erklärt: "Vor etwa zehn Jahren fing ich an, Weihnachtskrippen zu machen. Nach kurzer Zeit hörte ich auf, aber dann fing ich vor sieben Jahren wieder damit an." Solange sie sich erinnern kann, hat sie mit Ton gearbeitet. Sie wurde am 26. April 1932 als Tochter von Louis Loretto, einem Jemez-Indianer, und der aus Laguna-Pueblo stammenden Carrie Reid geboren. Sie besuchte die San Diego-Missionsschule, und während der Ferien half sie ihrer Mutter und Großmutter beim Töpfern. "Das erste, was ich mit zehn Jahren selber schuf, waren kleine Figürchen — Frauen mit einem oder zwei Babys in den Armen und dann Figuren in Kanus; ich gab jeder Gestalt einen Namen, wie zum Beispiel 'Sitting Bull'. Später fertigte ich Schüsseln und Hochzeitsvasen an."

Als sie Onofre Trujillo heiratete und nach Cochiti umzog, durfte sie den Ton aus Jemez nicht mehr benutzen, da jedes Pueblo seinen Ton für den eigenen Gebrauch innerhalb des Dorfes reserviert. Schließlich erhielt sie das Recht, den Ton aus Cochiti zu benutzen, und indem sie Onofres Tante Damacia Cordero töpfern half, lernte sie, diesen Ton zu bearbeiten. "Zunächst schuf ich Keramikformen, die genau wie die ihrigen aussahen, aber sie sagte mir, ich sollte sie auf meine eigene Weise gestalten, und das tat ich." Sie folgte der Tradition ihrer Verwandten mütterlicherseits und fertigte Töpfe und Wasserkrüge im Laguna Stil. "Dann

DOROTHY TRUJILLO es la mayor de seis hermanas, todas ceramistas y creadoras de Nacimientos. Ella dice, "Comencé a hacer Nacimientos hace aproximadamente diez años. Después de un tiempo paré, pero hace siete años los comencé a hacer otra vez." Ella ha trabajado con arcilla siempre, hasta donde tiene memoria. Nació en el pueblo Jemez el 26 de abril de 1932, y es la hija de Luis Loretto, originario de Jemez, y de Carrie Reid, del pueblo Laguna. Asistió a la Escuela Misionera de San Diego y pasó sus vacaciones ayudando a su madre y a su abuela en la creación de cerámicas. "Las primeras cosas que yo misma hice a los diez años fueron pequeñas figuras — mujeres con uno o dos bebés en los brazos y luego, figuras en canoas; a cada figura le ponía un nombre, como por ejemplo Sitting Bull. Más tarde hice vasijas y floreros de bodas."

Cuando se casó con Onofre Trujillo y se mudó a Cochiti, no le permitieron usar la arcilla de Jemez, ya que cada pueblo se reserva el derecho de emplear su propia arcilla dentro del pueblo. Eventualmente, le concedieron permiso para emplear las arcillas de Cochiti y aprendió a trabajar con ellas ayudándole a la tía de Onofre, Damacia Cordero. "Primero hice una cerámica como la de ella, pero más tarde ella me dijo que debía comenzar a crear mi propio estilo y así lo hice." Continuando la tradición del pueblo de su madre, hizo ollas y jarras de agua al estilo Laguna. "Luego

DOROTHY TRUJILLO   12-piece set
   1″ to 4½″ high   1977
The large, perfectly rounded heads on these
figures are one of Dorothy Trujillo's trademarks.
Other distinctive features of her sets are the
bold, crisp designs with which she decorates
the figures, the unusual shape of the cradle,
and her depiction of animals, such as this
donkey with its exaggerated long ears. Her
Three Wise Men bring gifts of rabbits, ears of
corn, and a platter of bread. Though she uses
Cochiti clay and the traditional Cochiti colors
of red and black, some details reflect her
native Jemez, such as the chongo knot hairstyle.
Museum of New Mexico Shop, Santa Fe,
New Mexico.

DOROTHY TRUJILLO   Gruppe von zwölf
   Figuren   2,5 bis 11,4 cm hoch   1977
Die großen, ganz runden Köpfe dieser Figuren
sind ein Warenzeichen Dorothy Trujillos.
Andere ausgeprägte Merkmale ihrer Gruppen
sind die kühnen, klaren Muster, mit denen sie
ihre Figuren verziert, die ungewöhnliche Form
der Wiege, und ihre Darstellung der Tiere,
beispielsweise des hier abgebildeten Esels
mit seinen übertrieben langen Ohren. Ihre drei
Weisen bringen Hasen, Maiskolben und eine
Schüssel mit Brot als Geschenke. Obwohl
sie Cochiti Ton und die traditionellen Cochiti
Farben Rot und Schwarz benützt, spiegeln ein
paar Einzelheiten ihr Heimat-Pueblo Jemez
wider, beispielsweise der Chongoknoten als
Haarstil. Verkaufsstelle des Museums von
New Mexico, Santa Fe, New Mexico.

DOROTHY TRUJILLO   juego de 12 piezas
   de 2.5 cm. a 11.4 cm. de alto   1977
Las cabezas grandes y perfectamente redondeadas de estas figuras son características
exclusivas de Dorothy Trujillo. Otras características sobresalientes de sus colecciones son
los diseños audaces y bien definido con los
cuales decora las figuras, la forma poco común
de la cuna, y la representación de animales,
como por ejemplo este burro de orejas exagera-
damente largas. Los Tres Reyes Magos traen
regalos: conejos, mazorcas de maíz, y una
bandeja de pan. Aunque emplea arcilla de
Cochiti y los colores tradicionales de Cochiti,
rojo y negro, algunos detalles reflejan aspectos
de su pueblo, Jemez, como por ejemplo el
moño de cabello al estilo "chongo." Tienda del
Museo de Nuevo México, Santa Fe.

people asked me if I made Storytellers. I made my first big one seven years ago, about the same time I started doing Nativities again." She has since won major prizes for both themes. In 1976 Saint Bonaventure Church in Cochiti asked her to make a large, brightly colored set, which was displayed in the church at Christmas.

Five of her six children are active in the crafts, and her husband makes silver and turquoise jewelry. They have built a shop in the back yard for the family's many creative enterprises. Dorothy teaches catechism to the children of the parish, and each Wednesday night she and Onofre hold a prayer meeting at their home for fifteen to thirty people. "We have our own family prayer time every evening, too. We can't do anything without the Lord's help, so we must give Him prime time."

fragten mich die Leute, ob ich Erzählerfiguren herstelle. Ich schuf meine erste große Erzählerfigur vor sieben Jahren, etwa zur selben Zeit, als ich wieder anfing, Weihnachtskrippen anzufertigen." Seitdem hat sie in beiden Kategorien größere Preise erhalten. Im Jahre 1976 hat die Saint Bonaventure-Kirche in Cochiti sie gebeten, eine große, bunte Gruppe zu schaffen, die dann zur Weihnachtszeit in der Kirche zur Schau gestellt wurde.

Fünf von ihren sechs Kindern sind als Kunsthandwerker tätig, und ihr Mann stellt Schmuck aus Silber und Türkis her. Im Garten haben sie einen Verkaufsladen für die vielen von der Familie geschaffenen Kunstwerke gebaut. Dorothy bringt den Kindern der Pfarrkirche den Katechismus bei, und jeden Mittwochabend findet eine Gebetversammlung für fünfzehn bis dreißig Leute in ihrem Haus statt. "Wir haben auch jeden Abend unsere eigene Familiengebetstunde. Ohne die Hilfe des Herrn können wir nichts machen; daher müssen wir ihm unsere beste Zeit widmen."

la gente me preguntó si yo hacía Narradores de Cuentos. Hice uno grande por primera vez hace siete años, aproximadamente en la misma época en que comencé a crear Nacimientos nuevamente." Desde entonces ha ganado premios importantes por ambos temas. En 1976, la Iglesia de San Buenaventura en Cochiti le pidió que creara un juego grande de colores brillantes el cual se exhibió en la iglesia en Navidad.

Cinco de sus seis hijos participan en artesanías, y su esposo hace joyería de plata y turquesa. Han construido un taller en el patio atrás de su casa para las varias actividades creativas de la familia. Dorothy les enseña el catecismo a los niños de la parroquia, y todos los miércoles de noche, ella y su esposo Onofre se reunen en su casa con quince a treinta personas para orar. "Cada noche, tenemos también nuestra propia hora familiar para orar. No podemos hacer nada sin la ayuda del Señor así que le debemos dar a Él tiempo especiál."

FELIPA TRUJILLO served a long apprenticeship in the pottery making craft. For most of her early life she helped her mother, the noted potter Stephanita Herrera, and much of Stephanita's pottery bears Felipa's finely drawn designs. It was not until 1960, after her mother died, that Felipa started making pottery on her own. She made bowls and the vessels with lizard spouts as her mother had done, but soon she was making more figures than bowls. "I had been doing figures for some time, and around 1969 some people who knew my work asked if I would make Nacimientos, and I said, 'Yes, I could try.' First I made Spanish-style sets; now I just make the Indian-style. The Spanish Nativities were done in the same colors and clay as the Indian, but the manger and the clothes were different. The people wore crowns, and the Virgin Mary wore an all-white dress. Last year I made about a dozen sets, all in the Indian style."

Born in Cochiti on April 27, 1908, Felipa attended Saint Catherine's School in Santa Fe, then married Paul Trujillo. They had six children and adopted another son. Like Felipa, Paul can claim a famous artist in the family,

FELIPA TRUJILLO ging lange in die Lehre, um die Töpferkunst zu erlernen. Während des größten Teils ihrer Jugend hat sie ihrer Mutter, der Töpferin Stephanita Herrera, geholfen, und viele Erzeugnisse Stephanitas zeigen die fein gezeichneten Muster Felipas. Erst im Jahre 1960, nach dem Tod ihrer Mutter, hat Felipa begonnen, ihre eigenen Töpferwaren herzustellen. Wie ihre Mutter, fertigte sie Schüsseln und Gefäße mit eidechsenförmigen Ausgüssen, aber bald schuf sie mehr Figuren als Schüsseln. "Ich hatte schon seit einiger Zeit Figuren gestaltet," erklärt sie, "und etwa 1969 fragten mich einige Leute, die meine Arbeiten kannten, ob ich *Nacimientos* machen würde, und ich erwiderte: 'Ja, ich könnte es versuchen.' Zunächst gestaltete ich Weihnachtsgruppen im spanischen Stil; jetzt mache ich sie nur noch im indianischen Stil. Die spanischen Weihnachtskrippen wurden in denselben Farben und demselben Ton wie die indianischen ausgeführt, aber die Krippe und die Kleider waren anders. Die Leute trugen Kronen, und die Heilige Jungfrau trug ein ganz weißes Kleid. Letztes Jahr stellte ich etwa ein Dutzend Gruppen her — alle im indianischen Stil."

Felipa wurde am 27. April 1908 in Cochiti geboren und ging zur Schule der Heiligen Katharina in Santa Fe. Dann heiratete sie Paul Trujillo. Sie hatten sechs Kinder und adoptierten noch einen Sohn. Wie Felipa, kann auch Paul sich rühmen, eine berühmte Künstlerin in seiner Familie zu haben, denn er

FELIPA TRUJILLO recibió un prolongado aprendizaje en el arte de la cerámica. La mayor parte de sus primeros años los pasó ayudando a su madre, la famosa ceramista Stephanita Herrera, y un gran parte de la cerámica de Stephanita lleva los diseños finamente dibujados de Felipa. No fue hasta 1960, después de la muerte de su madre, que Felipa comenzó a trabajar en la cerámica por su cuenta. Creó vasijas y ollas con cuellos de lagartijas, como la había hecho su madre, pero pronto se encontró creando más figuras que vasijas. "Por algún tiempo había hecho figuras, y aproximadamente en 1969, algunas personas que conocían mi trabajo, me preguntaron si podía hacer Nacimientos, y respondí que sí, que trataría. Primero hice juegos al estilo español; ahora los hago al estilo indio. Los Nacimientos españoles fueron realizados en el mismo color y arcilla que el de los indios, pero el pesebre y las ropas eran diferentes. La gente llevaba coronas y la Virgen María llevaba un vestido completamente blanco. El año pasado hice aproximadamente 12 juegos, todos al estilo indio."

Felipa nació en Cochiti el 27 de abril de 1908 y asistió a la Escuela Santa Catarina, en Santa Fe; luego se casó con Paul Trujillo. Tuvieron seis hijos y adoptaron uno más. Paul, como Felipa, también puede decir que un miembro de su

FELIPA TRUJILLO 13-piece set
  2¼″ to 5″ high 1975
One of the distinctive features of Felipa
Trujillo's Nativities is her cradle, a unique
interpretation of the Indian cradleboard. It
appears in most of her sets unless she has a
request for what she calls her "Spanish style,"
the traditional European crib of wood with
crossed legs. She usually includes one of her
Pueblo-style angels for which she is noted.
She says, "The Wise Men bring pottery and the
shepherds carry a lamb and a watermelon."
This set was featured in the December 1976
issue of *New Mexico* magazine. Mr. and Mrs.
Robert D. Davis, Santa Fe, New Mexico.

FELIPA TRUJILLO Gruppe von dreizehn
  Figuren 5,7 bis 12,7 cm hoch 1975
Eines der charakteristischen Merkmale der
Weihnachtskrippen Felipa Trujillos ist ihre
Wiege, eine einzigartige Auffassung der
Indianerwiege ("cradleboard"). Sie erscheint
in der Mehrzahl ihrer Gruppen, es sei denn,
jemand wünsche ihren "spanischen Stil" – die
traditionelle europäische Holzkrippe mit
gekreuzten Beinen. Gewöhnlich fügt sie einen
ihrer bekannten Engel im Pueblo-Stil den
anderen Figuren bei. Sie erklärt: "Die drei
Weisen bringen Töpferwaren und die Hirten
tragen ein Schaf und eine Wassermelone."
Diese Gruppe wurde in der Dezember 1976
Ausgabe der Zeitschrift *New Mexico*
abgebildet. Herr and Frau Robert D. Davis,
Santa Fe, New Mexico.

FELIPA TRUJILLO juego de 13 piezas
  de 5.7 cm. a 12.7 cm. de alto 1975
Una de las características sobresalientes de los
Nacimientos de Felipa Trujillo es la cuna, una
interpretación exclusiva de la cuna india.
Aparece en la mayor parte de sus colecciones
a menos que le pidan lo que ella llama "el estilo
español," la tradicional cuna europea de
madera con patas cruzadas. Sus Nacimientos
generalmente contienen uno de sus ángeles al
estilo "pueblo" por los cuales es afamada.
Felipa nos dice: "Los Tres Reyes Magos traen
piezas de cerámica, y los pastores llevan un
cordero y una sandía." Este juego se exhibió
en la publicación del mes de diciembre de 1976
de la revista *New Mexico*. Sr. y Sra. Robert D.
Davis, Santa Fe, Nuevo México.

for he is the uncle of Helen Cordero. Since his retirement from the New Mexico State Highway Department, he is able to devote more time to his own craft of drum making and to helping Felipa.

In addition to Nativities, Felipa is noted for her individual figures, which may range from two to fourteen inches high. Among her most popular themes are the mother and child, angels dressed in pueblo clothes, and stylized frogs with large open mouths — a traditional theme among Cochiti artists. Her larger figures include Storytellers and the Pottery Maker, a large seated woman holding a pot. For her figures, she uses a white clay that Paul gets for her from "a special place" around Cochiti and a red clay from La Bajada. He also helps with the tedious job of sanding the dried clay figures before firing. Both have won awards for their work at the Santa Fe Indian Market and the New Mexico State Fair.

ist der Onkel Helen Corderos. Seitdem er von seiner Arbeit beim New Mexico State Highway Department in den Ruhestand getreten ist, kann er seinem eigenen Kunsthandwerk — der Anfertigung von Trommeln — mehr Zeit widmen und Felipa helfen.

Außer für ihre Weihnachtskrippen ist Felipa für ihre Einzelgestalten bekannt, die 5 bis 35 cm hoch sind. Unter ihren beliebtesten Themen sind Mutter und Kind, in Pueblo-Tracht gekleidete Engel und stilisierte Frösche mit weit aufgerissenen Mäulern — ein traditionelles Thema der Künstler Cochitis. Unter ihren größeren Figuren findet man Erzähler und die Töpferin, eine große sitzende Frau, die einen Topf hält. Für ihre Figuren benutzt sie einen weißen Ton, den ihr Mann Paul von "einer besonderen Stelle" in der Nähe von Cochiti besorgt, und einen roten Ton aus La Bajada. Er hilft auch bei dem mühsamen Abschmirgeln der getrockneten Tonfiguren vor dem Brennen. Für ihr Kunsthandwerk haben beide Preise auf dem Santa Fe Indianermarkt und auf dem New Mexico Jahrmarkt erworben.

familia es famoso, porque es tío de Helen Cordero. Desde que se jubiló del Departamento de Carreteras del Estado de Nuevo México, puede dedicar más tiempo a su propio oficio: crear tambores y ayudar a Felipa.

Además de Nacimientos, Felipa es reconocida por sus figuras individuales que varían en tamaño de 5 a 35 centímetros de alto. Entre sus temas más populares se encuentran la madre y el niño, ángeles vestidos en ropas del pueblo, y ranas estilizadas con grandes bocas abiertas — uno de los temas tradicionales de los artistas de Cochiti. Entre sus figuras más grandes se hallan los Narradores de Cuentos y la Ceramista, una mujer de tamaño grande, sentada con una olla en la mano. Para crear sus figuras, emplea una arcilla blanca que Paul consigue "en un lugar especial" en los alrededores de Cochiti y una arcilla roja en La Bajada. También Paul le ayuda en el trabajo monótono de pulir las figuras de arcilla ya secas antes de cocerlas al fuego. Ambos han ganado premios por sus obras en el Mercado Indio de Santa Fe y en la Feria del Estado de Nuevo México.

JUANA LENO was inspired to make a Nativity one day in early 1976 when she was looking through her scrapbook and saw how much pottery she had made. "I thought of the things I had not made and one was a Nativity. That first year I made twelve sets and could not fill all my orders. For my Nativities, I use the same clay and fire them the same way as I do my pottery, but the modeling and painting of all the little figures takes longer."

Juana is ranked as a "Master Potter" at Acoma and has been working with clay "ever since I was old enough to play with it." She was born at Acomita on March 4, 1917, the daughter of Lupita and Jose Luis Vallo. Her mother was a potter and her paternal grandmother, Eulilia Vallo, was noted for her "Tularosa" design, which she had found on an ancient pottery shard. She passed the design on to Juana's mother, and now Juana uses it, too. Juana is noted for her "fine-line" pottery, featuring thin black lines thatched in intricate patterns, a technique she uses with great effect on her bowls, wedding vases, and distinctive three-chambered water jugs. She is also noted for her animal figures — owls, pigs, turtles — in a wide range of sizes. Sometimes tiny turtles will be

JUANA LENO kam auf den Gedanken, eine Weihnachtskrippe zu gestalten, als sie Anfang des Jahres 1976 in ihrem Sammelbuch blätterte und bemerkte, wie viele Töpferwaren sie bereits hergestellt hatte. "Ich fragte mich, welche Töpferwaren ich noch nicht produziert hatte, und dachte an eine Weihnachtskrippe. In jenem ersten Jahr schuf ich zwölf Gruppen, doch es war nicht möglich, alle Bestellungen zu erledigen. Ich benutze für meine Weihnachtskrippen denselben Ton und dieselbe Brenntechnik, wie für meine anderen Töpferwaren, aber das Modellieren und die Bemalung aller Figürchen nimmt mehr Zeit in Anspruch."

Juana gilt in Acoma als "Meistertöpferin" und arbeitet mit Ton "seitdem ich alt genug war, damit zu spielen." Sie wurde am 4. März 1917 als Tochter von Lupita und Jose Luis Vallo geboren. Ihre Mutter war Töpferin und ihre Großmutter väterlicherseits, Eulilia Vallo, war für ihr "Tularosa"-Muster bekannt, das sie auf einer prähistorischen Topfscherbe gefunden hatte. Dieses Muster hat sie an Juanas Mutter weitergegeben und jetzt macht auch Juana davon Gebrauch. Juana ist für ihre "dünn-liniierte" Töpferarbeit bekannt: dünne, schwarze Striche fließen in verwickelten Mustern ineinander, eine Technik, die sie sehr wirkungsvoll auf ihren Schüsseln, Hochzeitsvasen und dreihöhligen Wasserkrügen verwendet. Auch für ihre Tierfiguren ist sie bekannt — Eulen, Schweine, Schildkröten in verschiedenen Größen. Manchmal sitzen winzige Schildkrötlein auf dem Hals

JUANA LENO sintió la inspiración de crear un Nacimiento un día a principios de 1976 cuando se encontraba hojeando un álbum suyo y se dio cuenta de la cantidad de piezas de cerámica que ya había hecho. "Pensé en lo que aún no había realizado, y eso era un Nacimiento. En aquel primer año hice doce juegos y no puede cumplir con todos los pedidos. En mis Nacimientos empleo la misma arcilla y los cuezo al fuego de la misma forma que la cerámica que hago, pero la pintura y modelado de las pequeñas figuras requieren más tiempo."

Juana está considerada como una "Ceramista Magistral" en Acoma y ha trabajado con la arcilla "desde que tuve la edad suficiente para jugar con ella." Nació en Acomita, el 4 de marzo de 1917; es hija de Lupita y de José Luis Vallo. Su madre también era ceramista y su abuela paterna, Eulilia Vallo, fue bien conocida por el diseño "Tularosa," que había encontrado en un antiguo trozo de cerámica. La madre de Juana heredó el diseño, y ahora Juana lo usa también. Su obra llama la atención por las delicadas líneas de su cerámica, líneas finas y negras cruzadas, formando diseños complicados, una técnica muy eficaz que emplea en sus vasijas, jarrones de boda, y jarras originales de tres cavidades. También es bien conocida por sus figuras de animales — lechuzas, puercos, tortugas — en una amplia variedad de

JUANA LENO 13-piece set
1½″ to 3¼″ high 1976
Made in early 1976, this is different from the artist's later sets, where figures became more detailed, with defined legs. The Joseph and Mary figures here (left and right foreground) are closer in style to her more recent sets. The headbands and sashes are typical of Acoma. Of the donkey with the crossed black stripe on its back, Juana says, "The whole tribe paints them that way." She is one of the few artists to include a rooster in her sets. Here the Three Wise Men bear a platter of corn, wheat, and squash, and a pot and a drum. She notes: "The drum, along with a rattle, is played in our Christmas Eve Mass." Museum of Northern Arizona, Flagstaff, Arizona.

JUANA LENO Gruppe von dreizehn
Figuren 3,8 bis 8,3 cm hoch 1976
Diese 1976 gestaltete Gruppe unterscheidet sich von den späteren Gruppen der Künstlerin, in denen die Gestalten detaillierter und mit exakt modellierten Beinen ausgeführt werden. Die Figuren von Joseph und Maria (im linken und rechten Vordergrund) nähern sich mehr dem Stil der neueren Gruppen an. Die Kopfbinden und Schärpen sind für Acoma typisch. Von dem Esel mit dem gekreuzten schwarzen Streifen auf dem Rücken sagt Juana: "Der ganze Stamm bemalt sie so." Sie ist eine der wenigen Künstlerinnen, die ihren Gruppen auch einen Hahn beigibt. Hier tragen die drei Weisen einen Topf, eine Trommel und eine Schüssel mit Mais, Weizen und Kürbissen. Sie erklärt: "Die Trommel wird zusammen mit einer Rassel in unserer Weihnachtsmesse am Heiligen Abend gespielt." Verkaufsstelle des Museums von Northern Arizona, Flagstaff, Arizona.

JUANA LENO juego de 13 piezas
de 3.8 cm. a 8.3 cm. de alto 1976
Creado a principios de 1976, éste es diferente a los juegos que hizo más tarde en los cuales las figuras se volvieron más detalladas, con piernas más definidas. Las figuras de José y María aquí (en el primer plano, al derecho y a la izquierda) se parecen más cerca en estilo a sus más recientes. Las cintas de cabello y las fajas son típicas de Acoma. Juana explica, acerca del burro con líneas negras cruzadas sobre la espalda: "En toda la tribu los pintan así." Juana es uno de los pocos artistas que agrega un gallo a sus juegos. Aquí los Tres Reyes Magos llevan una bandeja con maíz, trigo, calabazas, una olla, y un tambor. Ella señala que "el tambor, junto con el sonajero, se tocan en la Misa del Gallo en Noche Buena." Museo del Norte de Arizona, Flagstaff, Arizona.

perched on the neck or top of her bowls.

She and her husband, Thomas, have ten children. Their five daughters — Rose, Phyllis, Marie, Isabel, and Regina — as well as their daughter-in-law, Joyce Leno, are all accomplished potters and help Juana tend her shop at old Acoma, which she operates each summer. Both Juana and Thomas are active in the Catholic church. Thomas is a sacristan and she is a member of the Legion of Mary, a group of church women who visit the sick and imprisoned. She has helped plaster the Acoma parish churches and has donated pottery to them. "When I was a child," she remembers, "the priest could come to Acoma only once a month. Now Father Sean takes care of our three churches, and we have Mass every Sunday. Though our Masses are in English, we pray in our own language, too. We are all created by one God, and all of our prayers go back to the same God."

eines Topfes oder zuoberst auf einer Schüssel.

Juana und ihr Mann Thomas haben zehn Kinder. Ihre fünf Töchter — Rose, Phyllis, Marie, Isabel und Regina — und auch ihre Schwiegertochter Joyce Leno — sind alle hervorragende Töpferinnen, die Juana jeden Sommer bei der Führung ihres Ladens in Alt-Acoma helfen. Sowohl Juana als auch Thomas sind aktive Mitglieder der katholischen Kirche in Acoma. Thomas ist Sakristan und Juana ist Mitglied der Marienschwestern (Legion of Mary), einer Gruppe von Frauen, die Kranke und Gefangene besuchen. Sie hat beim Verputzen der Pfarrkirchen in Acoma geholfen und Töpferwaren gestiftet. "Als ich ein Kind war", erinnert sie sich, "konnte der Priester nur einmal im Monat nach Acoma kommen. Jetzt betreut Pater Sean unsere drei Kirchen und wir haben jeden Sonntag eine Messe. Obwohl unsere Messen auf Englisch gehalten werden, beten wir auch in unserer eigenen Sprache. Wir wurden alle von einem Gott geschaffen, und unsere Gebete gehen zum selben Gott zurück."

tamaños. A veces se observan pequeñísimas tortugas colgadas del pescuezo o encima de sus vasijas.

Ella y su esposo, Thomas, tienen diez hijos. Sus cinco hijas — Rose, Phyllis, Marie, Isabel, y Regina — así como también su nuera, Joyce Leno, son ceramistas de grandes logros y le ayudan a Juana en la tienda que dirige los veranos en el viejo Acoma. Tanto Juana como Thomas participan de las actividades de la Iglesia Católica. Thomas es sacristán y ella es miembro de la Legión de María, un grupo de damas que visitan a los enfermos y a los prisioneros. Ella ha ayudado a enyesar las paredes de las parroquias de Acoma y ha donado a ellas algunas de sus piezas de cerámica. "Cuando era niña," recuerda, "el cura venía a Acoma solamente una vez al mes. Ahora Padre Sean se encarga de nuestras tres iglesias y tenemos misa todos los domingos. Aunque nuestras misas son en inglés, oramos en nuestra propia lengua también. Todos somos creados por un Dios, y todas nuestras oraciones se dirigen al mismo Dios."

ETHEL SHIELDS remembers helping her mother, Dolores Sanchez, with her pottery "when I was seventeen. We would load all the pottery into a wagon and drive to the main road between Grants and Albuquerque; that was before it was paved. We would sit there at a roadside stand and sell the pottery to people driving by." Ethel began making Nativity sets around 1975. "I started with the real tiny ones — figures about one-half inch to one inch high — and I have made hundreds of them since. In 1977 I started doing larger figures, too. I often make stables to go with my sets. Except for a wood floor, they are all of clay, with peaked steeple roofs and clay posts supporting them. Sometimes I use the all-wood stables that my sons make for me."

Among her other figurative pieces are Storytellers and, as she calls them, "my cradleboard babies." These are figures of the Baby Jesus in a cradleboard, about three inches long and two inches wide. "They are very popular, and I have 200 orders for them right now." She also makes unique tree ornaments: "They're little potteries, the size of golf balls, decorated with traditional designs." She likes doing large pots, about one foot high, decorated with traditional Acoma motifs; the part of the clay craft she most enjoys is

ETHEL SHIELDS erinnert sich, wie sie mit siebzehn Jahren ihrer Mutter Dolores Sanchez beim Töpfern geholfen hat. "Wir luden alle Tonwaren auf einen Wagen und fuhren zur Hauptstraße zwischen Grants und Albuquerque; damals war sie noch ungepflastert. Wir saßen dort in einem Verkaufsstand am Straßenrand und verkauften die Töpferwaren an die vorbeifahrenden Leute." Um 1975 begann Ethel, Weihnachtskrippen anzufertigen. "Ich fing mit winzig kleinen an — etwa 1,5 bis 2,5 cm hohe Figürchen — und seitdem habe ich Hunderte davon produziert. Seit 1977 fertige ich auch größere Figuren an. Ich mache auch Ställe für meine Gruppen. Mit Ausnahme des hölzernen Bodens sind sie ganz aus Ton, mit spitzen Dächern und Stützpfosten. Manchmal benutze ich hölzerne Ställe, die mir meine Söhne anfertigen."

Unter ihren anderen figürlichen Erzeugnissen befinden sich Erzähler und Figuren des Christkindes in der Wiege. Die letzteren, die sie "my cradleboard babies" nennt, sind etwa 7,6 cm lang und 5,1 cm breit. "Die Nachfrage ist sehr groß, und ich habe gerade jetzt 200 Bestellungen dafür." Sie fertigt auch einzigartigen Weihnachtsbaumschmuck an: "Es sind kleine Tonfigürchen, so groß wie Golfbälle, die mit traditionellen Mustern verziert werden." Sie gestaltet gerne große Töpfe, etwa dreißig cm hoch, die sie mit traditionellen Acoma Motiven verziert. Was ihr aber am besten gefällt, ist das Bemalen der Töpfer-

ETHEL SHIELDS recuerda cuando ayudaba a su madre Dolores Sánchez, con su cerámica "cuando tenía diez y siete años. Cargábamos todas las piezas de cerámica en una camioneta y manejábamos hasta el camino principal entre Grants y Albuquerque; éste era antes que lo fuera pavimentado. Nos sentábamos allí al lado del camino en un puesto y vendíamos las piezas de cerámica a los que pasaban en coche." Ethel comenzó a crear sus Nacimientos aproximadamente en 1975. "Comencé con las figuras pequeñitas — de 1.3 a 2.5 centímetros de alto — y he creado cientos de ellas desde entonces. En 1977 comencé a realizar figuras más grandes también. A menudo hago establos que van con mis juegos. Excepto por el piso de madera, todos son de arcilla con techos puntiagudos y postes de arcilla que los sostienen. A veces uso los establos totalmente de madera que mis hijos me construyen."

Entre sus otras piezas figurativas se encuentran los Narradores de Cuentos y, como ella misma los llama, "mis bebés de cunas portátiles." Estas son figuras del Niño Jesús en su cuna portátil de aproximadamente 7.6 centímetros de largo por 4.4 de ancho. "Son muy populares, y actualmente he recibido pedidos por 200 de ellos." También hace ornamentos originales para árboles: "Son pequeñas cerámicas, del tamaño de una pelota de golf, decoradas con diseños tradicionales." A ella le gusta crear ollas grandes, de aproximadamente 30 centímetros de alto, decoradas con motivos tradicionales de Acoma. El aspecto de la cerámica que más disfruta es la pintura.

ETHEL SHIELDS   6-piece set
   1¾" to 6" high   1977
The striking patterns on the garments of
Mary and Joseph are distinctive features. The
artist notes that they are typical of those on
the dance costumes worn for the annual
four-day Christmas ceremonies at Acoma, in
which she, herself, has danced. The white clay
and bright orange with black are also typical of
the fine pottery for which Acoma is noted.
In 1977 she made a set for herself, which has
been greatly admired. To the figures shown
here she added two angels and the Three Wise
Men and made a clay stable to house them.
Adobe Gallery, Albuquerque, New Mexico.

ETHEL SHIELDS   Gruppe von sechs
   Figuren   4,4 bis 15,2 cm hoch   1977
Die auffallenden Muster auf den Gewändern
Marias und Josephs sind charakteristische
Merkmale. Die Künstlerin erwähnt, daß diese
typisch sind für die Tanzkostüme, die bei den
jährlichen viertägigen Weihnachtszeremonien
in Acoma getragen werden, und daß sie
selbst an diesen Tänzen teilgenommen hat.
Auch der weiße Ton und die hellorange und
schwarze Bemalung charakterisieren die
feinen Töpferwaren, für die Acoma berühmt
ist. Im Jahre 1977 schuf Ethel für sich selbst
eine Weihnachtsgruppe, die man hochgepriesen
hat. Den hier abgebildeten Gestalten hat sie
noch zwei Engel und die drei Weisen
hinzugefügt und einen Tonstall gemacht, um
sie zu beherbergen. Adobe-Galerie,
Albuquerque, New Mexico.

ETHEL SHIELDS   juego de seis piezas
   de 5.1 cm. a 15.2 cm. de alto   1977
Los diseños llamativos de la ropa de María y
José constituyen características que resaltan.
La artista señala que son típicos de los vestidos
que los danzantes usan en la ceremonia anual
de Navidad en Acoma, que dura cuatro días
y en la que ella misma ha bailado. La arcilla
blanca y naranja brillante con negro es típica
de la cerámica por la cual Acoma es bien
conocida. En 1977, hizo un juego para ella
misma, que ha producido mucho admiración.
Agregó dos ángeles y los Tres Reyes Magos a
las figuras que aquí aparecen e hizo un establo
de arcilla en el cual las colocó. Galería Adobe,
Albuquerque, Nuevo México.

the painting. She uses an Acoma clay. "It is hard to get because it is in a cave, like a long tunnel, and you have to crawl on your stomach to get it."

Ethel was born in Acoma on September 17, 1926. After graduating from Albuquerque Indian School, she married Don Shields. They have eight children. The family lived in Tucson for twelve years, where Ethel worked in the Indian Center. Since their return to Acoma, and now that her children are older, she is devoting more time to her pottery. Her husband is a silversmith; one of her two daughters, Charmae, is a potter; a son, Jack, performs Indian dances. "Our family travels a lot to the Indian fairs and powwows, where Jack dances and we sell our crafts." When not traveling, they regularly attend Santa Maria Church in the Acoma village, McCarty's.

waren. Sie gebraucht Ton aus Acoma. "Es ist schwierig, an ihn heranzukommen, weil er in einer langen, tunnelartigen Höhle liegt; um ihn zu holen, muß man auf dem Bauch kriechen."

Ethel wurde am 17. September 1926 in Acoma geboren. Nachdem sie die Albuquerque Indianer-Schule absolviert hatte, heiratete sie Don Shields. Sie haben acht Kinder. Die Familie wohnte zwölf Jahre lang in Tucson, wo Ethel im Indian Center arbeitete. Da ihre Kinder jetzt älter sind, widmet sie seit ihrer Rückkehr nach Acoma der Töpferkunst mehr Zeit als früher. Ihr Mann ist Silberschmied, und eine ihrer zwei Töchter, die Charmae heißt, ist Töpferin; ein Sohn namens Jack führt indianische Tänze auf. "Unsere Familie reist viel zu den indianischen Jahrmärkten und Zeremonien, wo Jack tanzt und wir unser Kunsthandwerk verkaufen." Wenn sie nicht auf Reisen sind, gehen sie regelmäßig zur Santa Maria Kirche in dem Acoma-Indianerdorf McCarty's.

Emplea una arcilla de Acoma. "Es difícil conseguirla porque se halla en una cueva, parecida a un largo túnel, y hay que arrastrarse sobre el estómago para recogerla."

Ethel nació en Acoma el 17 de septiembre de 1926. Después de terminar sus estudios en la Escuela India de Albuquerque, se casó con Don Shields. Tienen ocho hijos. Por doce años vivieron en Tucson, donde Ethel trabajó en el Centro Indio. Desde que volvió a Acoma, y ahora que sus hijos son mayores, dedica más tiempo a su cerámica. Su esposo es platero; una de sus dos hijas, Charmae, es ceramista; su hijo Jack baila danzas indias. "Nuestra familia viaja mucho a las ferias indias y *Pow Wows*, donde Jack baila y nosotros vendemos nuestras artesanías." Cuando no viajan, asisten asiduamente a la Iglesia de Santa Maria en el pueblito de Acoma, McCarty's.

MARIE G. ROMERO is among the first potters in her pueblo to do Nativities. "It was something I wanted to try," she says. "I made my first set just before Christmas, 1975, and I was surprised when it sold immediately. The next August, I made some for the Santa Fe Indian Market and the opening of the Pueblo Cultural Center in Albuquerque, and the same thing happened. People wanted more; I had orders from all over the country." One of her sets took Second Prize at the Market that year, and in December one of her Nativities was pictured in *New Mexico* magazine. Her Storytellers, which she began making about 1972, are also very popular and have won awards. She is noted for other pottery pieces, particularly her innovative wedding vases and canteens with lizard handles.

Born in Jemez on July 27, 1927, the daughter of potter Persingula M. Gachupin, Marie began making and selling little Indian houses of clay when she was eight. "In those days our pottery was painted with showcard colors, which I never liked. Now I use natural colors fired in. Everything I use — the colors, the clay, and the fine sand — comes from Jemez." Following graduation from the Santa Fe Indian School,

MARIE G. ROMERO war eine der ersten Töpferinnen in ihrem Pueblo, die Weihnachtskrippen angefertigt haben. "Ich wollte es einmal versuchen," sagt sie. "Kurz vor Weihnachten 1975 machte ich meine erste Gruppe, und war erstaunt, als sie sofort gekauft wurde. Im folgenden August machte ich einige für den Santa Fe Indianermarkt und die Eröffnung des Pueblo-Kulturzentrums in Albuquerque, und dasselbe geschah. Die Leute wollten noch mehr kaufen, und ich erhielt Bestellungen aus allen Teilen des Landes." Eine ihrer Gruppen gewann in jenem Jahr den zweiten Preis beim Indianermarkt, und im Dezember wurde eine ihrer Weihnachtskrippen in der Zeitschrift *New Mexico* abgebildet. Ihre seit 1972 angefertigten Erzählerfiguren, die ebenfalls Preise erworben haben, sind sehr begehrt. Sie ist auch für andere keramische Erzeugnisse bekannt, insbesondere für ihre originellen Hochzeitsvasen und ihre mit eidechsenförmigen Handgriffen versehenen Feldflaschen.

Marie wurde am 27. Juli 1927 als Tochter der Töpferin Persingula M. Gachupin in Jemez geboren, und fing schon mit acht Jahren an, kleine Indianerhäuschen aus Ton zu gestalten und zu verkaufen. "Damals wurden unsere Tonwaren in Postkartenfarben bemalt, die mir nie gefallen haben. Heute benutze ich eingebrannte Naturfarben. Alles, was ich benutze — die Farben, der Ton, und der feine Sand — kommt aus Jemez." Nachdem sie die Santa Fe Indianer-Schule absolviert

MARIE G. ROMERO es una de las primeras ceramistas de su pueblo en crear Nacimientos. "Era algo que deseaba probar," dice. "Hice mi primer juego un poco antes de la Navidad, en 1975, y me sorprendí cuando se vendió inmediatamente. El siguiente agosto, hice algunos para el Mercado Indio de Santa Fe y para la inauguración del Centro Cultural Pueblo en Albuquerque, y sucedió lo mismo. La gente quería más; recibí pedidos de todas partes del país." Uno de sus juegos recibió el Segundo Premio en el Mercado ese año, y en diciembre uno de sus Nacimientos apareció en la revista *New Mexico*. Sus Narradores de Cuentos, que comenzó aproximadamente en 1972, son también muy conocidos y han sido premiados. Esta artista se distingue por otras piezas de cerámica, especialmente sus originales floreros de bodas y cantimploras con mangos en forma de lagartija.

Nació en Jemez, el 27 de julio de 1927, hija de la ceramista Persíngula M. Gachupín, Marie comenzó a hacer y vender casitas indias de arcilla a la edad de ocho años. "En esa época, nuestra cerámica estaba pintada con colores chillones que nunca me gustaron. Ahora uso colores naturales, al fuego. Todo lo que uso — los colores, la arcilla, y la arena fina — son de Jemez." Después de terminar los cursos en la Escuela India

MARIE G. ROMERO   9-piece set
  1¾″ to 4½″ high   1977
Distinctive features of this artist's Nativities
are the patterned shawls and robes. Sometimes
she does them all in stripes; here they are
reminiscent of Pendleton blanket designs. In her
most recent sets she has added a donkey with
a patterned saddle blanket. The angel figure
(far left); the Three Wise Men bearing gifts of
pottery, bread, and ears of corn; the Jemez-
style cradleboard; chongo knot hairstyles; and
happy smiles on the faces are consistent
features of her sets. The sheep and shepherd
are designed so that the shepherd's hand
can rest on the sheep's back.
Authors' Collection, Flagstaff, Arizona.

MARIE G. ROMERO   Gruppe von neun
  Figuren   4,4 bis 11,4 cm hoch   1977
Charakteristisch für die Weihnachtskrippen
dieser Künstlerin sind die gemusterten Schals
und Roben. Manchmal gestaltet sie diese ganz
in Streifen; hier erinnern sie an das Muster
der Pendleton-Decken. Ihren neuesten Gruppen
hat sie einen Esel mit eine gemusterten
Satteldecke hinzugefügt. Der Engel (weit links);
die drei Weisen, die Töpferwaren, Brot und
Maiskolben als Geschenke bringen; die Wiege
("cradleboard") im Jemez Stil; in Chongoknoten
geflochtene Haare und das glückliche Lächeln
auf den Gesichtern sind typische Merkmale
ihrer Gruppen. Das Schaf und der Hirt werden
so gestaltet, daβ die Hand des Hirten auf
dem Rücken des Schafes ruhen kann.
Sammlung der Autoren, Flagstaff, Arizona.

MARIE G. ROMERO   juego de 9 piezas
  de 4.4 cm. a 11.4 cm. de alto   1977
Una de las características sobresalientes de los
Nacimientos de esta artista son los chales y
túnicas adornada con diseños. A veces los hace
todas con rayadas; aquí nos recuerdan a los
diseños de las mantas Pendleton. En sus juegos
más recientes ha agregado un burro con una
manta de montar adornada con diseños. La
figura del ángel (atrás a la izquierda); los Tres
Reyes Magos trayendo regalos de cerámica, pan,
y mazorcas de maíz; la cuna portátil, al estilo
Jemez; moños de estilo "chongo"; y rostros
sonrientes son las características constantes de
sus juegos. La oveja y el pastor están diseñados
de tal forma que la mano de éste puede
descansar sobre el lomo de la oveja. De la
colección de los autores, Flagstaff, Arizona.

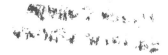

50

Marie worked in a gift shop in Phoenix, Arizona, and later took courses in art and early childhood education from the University of New Mexico and the University of Albuquerque. For many years she has taught daily classes in clay at the Jemez Day School. Her daughters, Maxine R. Toya and Laura Gachupin, are also accomplished potters, and Maxine has given pottery demonstrations with her mother at various schools.

Both Marie and her husband, Leonard, attend San Diego Mission Catholic Church and take part in the big feast days of the pueblo — San Diego Feast Day on November 12 and the Feast Day of the Pecos on August 2, which is also the Feast Day of Saint Persingula, for whom her mother was named. "There are dances on Easter Sunday too, but the longest celebration of the year is the one at Christmas. It begins with Mass on Christmas Eve and runs through January 6, the Day of the Three Kings."

hatte, arbeitete Marie in einem Laden in Phoenix, Arizona, und studierte später Kunst und Kinderpädagogik an der Universität von New Mexico und der Universität von Albuquerque. Seit vielen Jahren unterrichtet sie täglich Keramikklassen an der Jemez-Tagesschule. Auch ihre Töchter Maxine A. Toya und Laura Gachupin sind ausgezeichnete Töpferinnen. Maxine und ihre Mutter haben die Töpferkunst an verschiedenen Schulen vorgeführt.

Sowohl Marie als auch ihr Mann Leonard sind Mitglieder der katholischen Missionskirche des Heiligen Diego und nehmen an den groβen Festtagen des Pueblos teil — dem Festtag des Heiligen Diego am 12. November und dem Pecos-Festtag am 2. August. Dieser ist auch der Festtag der Heiligen Persingula, nach der ihre Mutter genannt wurde. "Auch am Ostersonntag gibt es Tänze, aber der längste Tanz des Jahres ist das Weihnachtsfest. Es beginnt mit der Weihnachtsmesse und dauert bis zum 6. Januar, dem Fest der Heiligen Drei Könige."

de Santa Fe, Marie trabajó en una tienda de regalos en Phoenix, Arizona, y más tarde asistió a clases de arte y de la educación temprana del niño en la Universidad de Nuevo México y en la Universidad de Albuquerque. Por muchos años ha dictado cursos de cerámica en la Escuela Diurna de Jemez. Sus hijas, Maxine R. Toya y Laura Gachupín, también son ceramistas consumadas, y Maxine con su madre han realizado demostraciones en varias escuelas.

Marie y su esposo Leonard asisten a la Misión Católica de San Diego y participan en los días festivos más importantes del pueblo: el día festivo de San Diego, el 12 de noviembre, y el 2 de agosto, el día festivo de Pecos, que es también el día de Santa Persíngula por quien fue nombrada la madre de ella. El Domingo de Resurrección también hay danzas, pero la festividad que dura más es la Navidad. Comienza con la Misa del Gallo de Noche Buena y continua hasta el 6 de enero, el día de los Tres Reyes Magos."

NAVAJO TRIBE

TOM W. YAZZIE is a prize-winning woodcarver who is noted for his representations of Navajo ceremonies and daily life. He believes he carved his first Nativity about fifteen years ago. Though he has made only four sets, their record is impressive; one was exhibited at the Wheelwright Museum, Santa Fe; another is in the permanent collection of the Navajo Tribal Museum in Window Rock, Arizona; one took a Second Award at the 1968 Scottsdale National Indian Arts Exhibition; the most recent won a First Award at the 1978 Inter-Tribal Indian Ceremonial at Gallup, New Mexico. The last had been commissioned by a well-known Dutch collector, Dr. Maria Elizabeth Houtzager. Tom notes: "She came all the way from Holland to pick up the set and will show it in a Nativities exhibit she is planning in Europe."

Yazzie was born on July 25, 1930, on the Navajo reservation at Fort Defiance, Arizona, and attended Fort Defiance Boarding School. From 1947 to 1954, he served with the United States Army in the First Division and later with the Rangers. "When I was a soldier in Europe, on our endless marches, I would often pick up a twig and carve it with

TOM W. YAZZIE ist ein Holzschnitzer, der viele Preise erworben hat, und der wegen seiner Darstellungen von Zeremonien und Szenen aus dem täglichen Leben der Navajo-Indianer bekannt ist. Er glaubt, daß er seine erste Weihnachtskrippe vor ungefähr fünfzehn Jahren geschnitzt habe. Obwohl er nur vier Gruppen angefertigt hat, haben alle Erfolg gehabt: eine wurde im Wheelwright Museum in Santa Fe ausgestellt; eine andere befindet sich in der Dauerausstellung des Navajo Tribal Museums in Window Rock, Arizona; im Jahre 1968 erhielt eine seiner Krippen den zweiten Preis in der Nationalausstellung indianischer Künste in Scottsdale, Arizona; und die neueste Weihnachtskrippe hat 1978 den ersten Preis beim Inter-Tribal Indian Ceremonial in Gallup, New Mexico, erworben. Diese war von einer bekannten niederländischen Sammlerin, Dr. Maria Elizabeth Houtzager, bestellt worden. Tom erklärt: "Sie reiste sogar von Holland hierher, um die Weihnachtsgruppe abzuholen, und wird sie in einer von ihr geplanten Weihnachtskrippenausstellung in Europa zeigen."

Yazzie wurde am 25. Juli 1930 auf der Navajo-Reservation in Fort Defiance, Arizona, geboren, und war Schüler im dortigen Internat. Von 1947 bis 1954 diente er in der ersten Division und später bei den *Rangers* der amerikanischen Armee. "Als wir während meiner Soldatenzeit in Europa die endlosen Märsche machten, nahm ich oft einen Zweig vom Boden auf und schnitzte ihn mit meinem Bajonett.

TOM W. YAZZIE es un tallador de madera premiado en varios ocasiones quien es bien conocido por sus representaciones de las ceremonias y escenas de la vida cotidiana de los Navajos. Cree haber tallado su primer Nacimiento aproximadamente hace quince años. Aunque solamente ha creado cuatro juegos, sus prestigio es impresionante: uno se exhibió en el Museo Wheelwright de Santa Fe; otro se encuentra en la exposición permanente del Museo de la Tribu Navajo en Window Rock, Arizona; otro recibió el Segundo Premio en la Exhibición Nacional de Arte Indio de Scottsdale en 1968; el más reciente recibió el Primer Premio en el Ceremonial Indio Intertribu, 1978, en Gallup, Nuevo México. Este último había sido encomendado por una bien conocida coleccionista holandesa, la Dra. María Elizabeth Houtzager. Tom señala, "Ella vino desde Holanda para llevarse el juego que mostrará en una exhibición de Nacimientos que planea presentar en Europa."

Yazzie nació el 25 de julio de 1930, en la Reservación Navajo en el Fort Defiance, Arizona, y estudió en la escuela internada del mismo lugar. Entre 1947 y 1954, estuvo con el ejército de los Estados Unidos, en la Primera División y más tarde con los comandos. "Cuando era soldado en Europa, en esas marchas interminables, solía recoger una ramita y la tallaba con la bayoneta. En mi tiempo libre también tallaba la madera, porque

TOM W. YAZZIE   12-piece set
  2½″ to 10″ high   ca. 1964
The collector notes that this set received a
Second Award at the Scottsdale National
Indian Arts Exhibition in 1968. Yazzie believes
it is the first set he did, which would date
it around 1964. He says, "It is the only one of
my sets that has a donkey, and in the other
sets I have three shepherds instead of two."
Here the two shepherds, as well as the Three
Wise Men, bring gifts — silver, turquoise, and
sacred corn meal. Like most of his figures, these
are carved in cottonwood root and painted,
with a fine attention to detail and authenticity.
Jean Seth, Santa Fe, New Mexico.

TOM W. YAZZIE   Gruppe von zwölf
  Figuren   6,4 bis 25,4 cm hoch   ca. 1964
Der Sammler erklärt, daβ diese Gruppe 1968
einen zweiten Preis in der Nationalausstellung
indianischer Künste in Scottsdale, Arizona,
erhalten hat. Yazzie glaubt, daβ dies seine
erste Gruppe ist, die er um 1964 geschaffen hat.
Er sagt: "Sie ist die einzige meiner Weihnachtsgruppen, die einen Esel hat, und in den
anderen Gruppen habe ich drei Hirten anstatt
zwei." Hier tragen die zwei Hirten, wie auch
die drei Weisen, Geschenke — Silber, Türkis
und geweihtes Maismehl. Wie die meisten
seiner Figuren, wurden auch diese mit
groβer Sorgfalt für Einzelheiten und Echtheit
aus Pappelwurzeln geschnitzt und bemalt.
Jean Seth, Santa Fe, New Mexico.

TOM W. YAZZIE   juego de 12 piezas
  de 6.4 cm. a 25.4 cm. de alto   circa 1964
El coleccionista señala que este juego recibió
el Segundo Premio en la Exposición Nacional
de Arte Indio de Scottsdale en 1968. Yazzie
cree que esta es el primer juego que hizo, que
sería aproximadamente en 1964. Dice: "Es la
única de mis juegos que tiene un burro; y en
los otros juegos he puesto tres pastores en lugar
de dos." Aquí los dos pastores, así como
también los Tres Reyes Magos, traen regalos:
plata, turquesa, y la harina de maíz sagrada.
Como la mayoría de sus figuras, éstas son
talladas en raíces de álamo y pintadas con gran
atención en todos sus detalles y autenticidad.
Jean Seth, Santa Fe, Nuevo México.

53

my bayonet. I carved in my spare time too, because the Germans were very interested in Indian crafts. Then, when I returned and became boys' advisor at the Fort Defiance School, I met a teacher, another German, Jack Schwanke, who carved puppets, and he got me interested in carving again." These early carvings were smaller and were decorated with beads, feathers, ribbons, and tin ornaments. Now ornamentation is carved on his pieces and painted. He works primarily in cottonwood root, which he finds "walking along the arroyos here or while plowing for my neighbors." He uses a few simple tools — a small saw, a pick, a rasp, and an X-acto knife. Since he works full time as a millwright at the Navajo Forest Products Industry, he does his carving in the evening. His wife Marie paints his pieces, and his son Vernon, one of their seven children, often carves with him. In early 1979, he had a one-man exhibition in Lakewood, Colorado.

Auch in meiner Freizeit habe ich Holzschnitzereien gemacht, weil die Deutschen viel Interesse für indianisches Kunsthandwerk zeigten. Als ich dann nach Arizona zurückkehrte und Berater der Schüler in Fort Defiance wurde, lernte ich Jack Schwanke kennen, einen deutschen Lehrer, der Marionetten schnitzte, und er erweckte in mir wiederum das Interesse an der Holzschnitzerei." Diese frühen Holzschnitzarbeiten waren kleiner und waren mit Perlen, Federn, Bändern und Blechschmuck verziert. Heute wird die Verzierung in seine Kunstobjekte eingeschnitzt und bemalt. Er arbeitet in erster Linie mit Pappelwurzeln, die er entdeckt, "wenn ich am trockenen Flußbett (*arroyo*) entlanggehe oder wenn ich die Felder meiner Nachbarn pflüge." Er gebraucht nur einige einfache Werkzeuge — eine kleine Säge, eine Raspel und ein X-acto-Taschenmesser. Da er tagsüber als Mechaniker bei der Navajo-Forstwirtschaftsindustrie arbeitet, betreibt er die Holzschnitzarbeit am Abend. Seine Frau Marie bemalt seine Schnitzereien, und sein Sohn Vernon, eines ihrer sieben Kinder, schnitzt oft mit ihm zusammen. Am Anfang des Jahres 1979 veranstaltete er eine Einmannausstellung in Lakewood, Colorado.

a los alemanes les interesaban las artesanías de los indios. Luego, cuando volví y me convertí en consejero de jóvenes de la Escuela Fort Defiance, conocí a un maestro alemán, Jack Schwanke, que hacía marionetas, y me entusiasmó para que tallara la madera nuevamente." Los primeros trabajos eran más pequeños y estaban decorados con lentejuelas, plumas, cintas, y ornamentos de lata. Ahora cada parte del ornamento está tallada y pintada. Trabaja principalmente con raíces de álamos que encuentra "caminando por las orillas de los arroyos aquí o cuando aro las tierras de mis vecinos." Usa pocas herramientas sencillas: un serrucho pequeño, un pico, un raspador, y un estilete. Porque trabaja todo el tiempo como constructor de molinos en la Empresa Industrial Navajo de Productos Forestales, realiza sus trabajos artísticos por la noche. Su esposa Marie pinta las figuras, y uno de sus siete hijos, Vernon, trabaja con él a menudo. A principios de 1979 presentó una exhibición en Lakewood, Colorado.

DOMINGO AND CHEPA FRANCO, a husband-and-wife team, worked together for over forty years creating scenes of Papago daily life. Domingo carved figures of people and animals, and Chepa added the decorative touches. They did single figures and groups, often setting them in ramadas or in the grass-thatched huts that were the dwellings of the Papagos in ancient times. Most of their materials came from the Arizona desert around them — saguaro cactus ribs for the figures, mesquite branches, dried grasses, and fine gravel for the ramadas. Chepa dried fruit stones and painted them to look like real fruit — apricot stones became watermelons and peach stones became cantaloupes. Friends supplied the rest — scraps of fabric for the clothes, wire coat hangers to make frames for the burden baskets some figures carry on their backs. One friend brings wigs from Tucson beauty salons, which Chepa cuts into tiny hair pieces. "We never use nylon wigs," she says, "only real hair."

Both were born on the Papago reservation: Domingo at San Xavier in the late 1880s, and Chepa in the village of Pan Tak on June 24, 1901. Following their marriage they settled in Domingo's village, which clusters around the historic San Xavier Mission. Domingo displayed an interest and talent in art from early childhood. For a time he

DOMINGO UND CHEPA FRANCO arbeiteten über vierzig Jahre lang gemeinsam an der Gestaltung von Szenen aus dem Alltag der Papago-Indianer. Domingo schnitzte Menschen- und Tiergestalten, und Chepa sorgte für die Ausschmückung. Sie fertigten Einzelfiguren und Gruppen und setzten sie oft in Ramadas oder in mit Gras bedeckte Hütten, die in vergangenen Zeiten den Papagos als Wohnhäuser dienten. Sie verwendeten größtenteils Werkstoffe aus der sie umgebenden Wüste Arizonas — Saguaro-Kaktusrippen für die Gestalten; Mesquite-Äste, getrocknete Gräser und feinen Kies für die Ramadas. Chepa dörrte Obststeine und bemalte sie so, daß sie wie wirkliches Obst aussahen — Pfirsich- und Aprikosensteine wurden zu Melonen und Wassermelonen. Ihre Freunde sorgten für andere Stoffe — Gewebereste für die Kleider, Drahtkleiderbügel für die Rahmen der Kiepen, die manche Figuren auf dem Rücken tragen. Aus Schönheitssalons in Tucson brachte eine der Freundinnen Perücken, die Chepa zu winzigen Haartrachten zuschnitt. "Wir gebrauchen nie Nylonperücken", erklärt sie, "nur echte Haare."

Die beiden wurden in dem Papago-Reservat geboren: Domingo gegen Ende der 80er Jahre des 19. Jahrhunderts in San Xavier, und Chepa am 24. Juni 1901 im Dorf Pan Tak. Nach ihrer Hochzeit zogen sie in Domingos Heimatdorf, das die historische San Xavier-Missionskirche umgibt. Seit seiner Kindheit zeigte Domingo Interesse und Begabung für die Kunst. Eine

DOMINGO Y CHEPA FRANCO, casados, trabajaron juntos por más de cuarenta años creando escenas de la vida cotidiana de los Pápagos. Domingo talló figuras de la gente y de los animales, y Chepa hizó los toques decorativos. Crearon figuras individuales y en grupos, muchos colocados en ramadas o en las chozas con techos de paja, los hogares de los antiguos Pápagos. Empleaban muchos materiales de los alrededores en el desierto de Arizona: los nervios del cactos saguaro para las figuras, y ramitas de mezquite, hierba seca, y grava fina para las ramadas. Chepa secaba huesos de fruta y los pintaba para que parecieran frutas verdaderas: los huesos de albaricoques se convertían en sandías y los de melocotones se convertían en melones. Sus amigos le proveían los demás materiales: pedazos de tela para la ropa, perchas de alambre para hacer los esqueletos de cestas que algunas figuras cargan en la espalda. Un amigo trae pelucas de las peluquerías en Tucson, y Chepa las corta y hace con ellas pequeñas pelucas. Ella dice: "Nunca usamos pelucas de nylon, sólo de pelo natural."

Ambos nacieron en la Reservación Pápago: Domingo nació en San Xavier hacia fines de 1880, y Chepa nació en el pueblo Pan Tak el 24 de julio de 1901. Después de su casamiento se mudaron al pueblo nativo de Domingo, que se agrupa alrededor de la Misión histórica de San Xavier. Domingo demostró interés y habilidad para las artes desde su infancia. Por cierto tiempo hizo tambores y juegos de arco y flecha para una

made drums and bow-and-arrow sets for a curio store in Tucson. Then he started carving animals out of saguaro cactus ribs to be attached to the base of lamps made of the ribs by a man in Tucson. Chepa cut parchment and laced it for the lampshades, and on these Domingo painted designs and desert scenes. Eventually he began carving people as well as animals, and this was the beginning of their unique creations of Papago life.

They did their first Nativity in the early 1960s when Father Camillus Cavagnaro commissioned one for the San Jose Mission Church in Pisinemo village. For it they used the same materials they had used for their Papago life scenes. A mobile for the hanging angels was specially designed by Papago artist Frank Mariano. Other Nativities were ordered; in 1965 the Arizona State Museum commissioned them to make one for their permanent collection. It was completed just before Domingo's death on May 22, 1966. Chepa says, "When Domingo died, I felt so bad I couldn't do anything. Everyone encouraged me to make the figures like Domingo did, but I didn't know if I could. Then a friend at the Arizona State Museum told me I must start again, and I began to try carving and found I could do it." Now she does both

Zeitlang fertigte er Trommeln, Pfeile und Bogen für einen Kuriositätenladen in Tucson an. Dann begann er, aus Saguaro-Kaktusrippen Tiere zu schnitzen, die am Fuße der Lampen befestigt wurden, die ein Tucsoner aus dem gleichen Material anfertigte. Chepa schnitt und formte Pergament für die Lampenschirme, die Domingo mit Mustern und Wüstenszenen bemalte. Schließlich begann er, Menschen- und Tiergestalten zu schnitzen; das war der Anfang ihrer einzigartigen Nachbildungen des Papago-Lebens.

Sie schufen ihre erste Weihnachtskrippe zu Beginn der sechziger Jahre, als Pater Camillus Cavagnaro eine Weihnachtskrippe für die San Jose-Missionskirche im Dorf Pisinemo in Auftrag gab. Dafür verwendeten sie dieselben Materialien, wie für ihre Szenen aus dem Papago-Leben. Ein Mobile für die schwebenden Engel wurde zu diesem Zweck von dem Papago-Künstler Frank Mariano speziell entworfen. Weitere Weihnachtskrippen wurden bestellt, und im Jahre 1965 hat das Arizona State Museum die Francos beauftragt, eine Weihnachtskrippe für seine Dauersammlung herzustellen. Sie wurde kurz vor dem Tode Domingos am 22. Mai 1966 vollendet. Chepa sagt: "Als Domingo starb, war ich so traurig, daß ich nichts anfangen konnte. Jedermann ermutigte mich, Figuren so zu bilden, wie Domingo es getan hatte, aber ich wußte nicht, ob ich es konnte. Dann sagte mir ein Freund vom Arizona State Museum, ich müsse wieder zu arbeiten anfangen; ich versuchte zu schnitzen, und es gelang

tienda en Tucson. Después comenzó a tallar animales de los nervios de cactos unidos a la base de lámparas que un hombre en Tucson hacía de los mismos nervios. Chepa cortaba pergamino y lo entrelazaba para las pantallas, y entonces Domingo las pintaba con diseños y paisajes del desierto. Eventualmente, empezó a tallar figuras humanas así como también de animales, y éste fue el origen de sus representaciones de la vida de los Pápago.

Hicieron su primer Nacimiento a principios de 1960 cuando el Padre Camillus Cavagnaro encargó uno para la iglesia de la Misión de San José en el pueblo Pisinemo. Lo hicieron empleando los mismos materiales que usaron para sus escenas de la vida diaria de su tribu. El artista Pápago, Franco Mariano, diseñó exclusivamente para ellos una pieza movible para los ángeles pendientes. Se encargaron otros Nacimientos; en 1965 el Museo del Estado de Arizona les pidió que hicieran uno para su colección permanente. Lo terminaron poco antes de que Domingo muriera el 22 de mayo en 1966. Dice Chepa: "Cuando murió Domingo, me sentí tan triste que no pude hacer nada. Todos me animaron para que creara figuras así como lo había hecho Domingo, pero no sabía si podría hacerlo. Después, un amigo que trabajaba en el Museo del Estado de Arizona insistió en que comenzara nuevamente, y empecé a tratar de tallar figuras y me di cuenta de que podía hacerlo." Ahora hace las dos cosas, el tallado y los últimos

DOMINGO AND CHEPA FRANCO
7-piece set   4″ to 10″ high   1966
Arizona State Museum commissioned the
Francos to do this set in 1965. It was the last
thing Domingo did — completed just before his
death in 1966. The set is housed in the ramada
type of structure made of mesquite wood
that the Francos used for their scenes of Papago
daily life. The ollas hanging from the roof
and the jugs on the floor are also typical
touches. When viewed in the museum display,
the archway in the adobe brick wall reveals
a scene of San Xavier Mission. The figures were
carved in saguaro cactus rib by Domingo and
clothed by Chepa. Arizona State Museum,
University of Arizona, Tucson.

DOMINGO UND CHEPA FRANCO   Gruppe
von sieben Figuren   10,2 bis 25,4 cm hoch
1966
Das Arizona State Museum in Tucson hat die
Francos im Jahre 1965 beauftragt, diese
Gruppe anzufertigen. Es war Domingos
letztes Werk, das er kurz vor seinem Tode
im Jahre 1966 vollendete. Die Gruppe befindet
sich in einem Ramada-artigen Bau aus
Mesquite-Holz, den die Francos für ihre
Szenen aus dem täglichen Leben der Papago-
Indianer verwendeten. Typisch sind auch
die vom Dach hängenden Wasserkrüge (*ollas*)
und die Krüge auf dem Boden. Betrachtet man
diese Gruppe in der Ausstellung des
Museums, so erblickt man durch das Tor in
der Adobe-Ziegelmauer eine Darstellung der
San Xavier-Missionskirche. Die Gestalten
wurden von Domingo aus Saguaro-Kaktusrippen geschnitzt und von Chepa mit
Kleidern versehen. Arizona State Museum,
Universität von Arizona, Tucson, Arizona.

DOMINGO Y CHEPA FRANCO   juego de
7 piezas   de 10.2 cm. a 25.4 cm. de alto
1966
El Museo del Estado de Arizona comisionó a
los esposos Franco para que hicieran este juego
en 1965. Fue la última creación de Domingo —
terminada poco antes de su fallecimiento en
1966. El juego está albergado en la ramada
hecha de mezquite que los Franco usaron para
sus escenas de la vida diaria de los Pápagos.
Las ollas que cuelgan del techo y los jarros en
el piso son toques típicos. Cuando se observa
en la exposición del museo, la arcada en la
pared de ladrillo adobe revela una escena de la
Misión de San Xavier. Las figuras las talló
Domingo del nervio del cactos saguaro, y
Chepa fue la encargada de vestirlas.
Museo del Estado de Arizona,
Universidad de Arizona, Tucson.

DOMINGO AND CHEPA FRANCO
16-piece set   6″ to 14″ high   ca. 1963
This was the Francos' first Nativity. It was
commissioned for San Jose Church and kept as
a surprise for Christmas Eve. The Nativity
was placed on the altar; above it the angels
were suspended from a mobile lighted with
candles, which kept the angels in constant
motion. Music piped in from above made it
seem as if the angels' tiny flute and violin were
producing the sound. As Chepa says, "There
were many stiff necks from looking up so
much." On January 6, the Three Wise Men
joined the other figures on the altar. All of the
figures are carved out of saguaro cactus ribs;
some of the people are jointed at the waist
to bend in reverence. San Jose Mission,
Pisinemo, Arizona.

DOMINGO UND CHEPA FRANCO   Gruppe
von sechzehn Figuren   15,2 bis 35,6 cm
hoch   ca. 1963
Die hier abgebildete Weihnachtskrippe war
die erste, die die Francos geschaffen haben.
Sie wurde von der San Jose-Kirche in Auftrag
gegeben und blieb ein Geheimnis bis zum
Heiligen Abend. Man stellte die Weihnachtskrippe auf den Altar; darüber wurden an
einem Mobile hängende Engel durch Kerzen
beleuchtet und in ständiger Bewegung gehalten.
Von oben her erklang Musik; es war als ob die
Engel selber auf der kleinen Flöte und Geige
spielten. Chepa bemerkt: "Viele Hälse wurden
vom vielen Hinaufschauen steif." Am 6. Januar
gesellten sich die drei Weisen zu den anderen
Gestalten auf dem Altar. Alle Menschengestalten sind aus Saguaro-Kaktusrippen
geschnitzt; manche sind in der Taille mit
Gelenken versehen, um sich in Ehrerbietung
verbeugen zu können. San Jose-Missionskirche,
Pisinemo, Arizona.

DOMINGO Y CHEPA FRANCO   juego de
16 piezas   de 15.2 cm. a 35.6 cm. de alto
circa 1963
Este fue el primer Nacimiento de los esposos
Franco. Les fue comisionado por la Iglesia de
San José y se guardó como una sorpresa para la
Noche Buena. El Nacimiento se puso en el altar;
arriba de lo, se colocó una pieza movible
iluminada con velas, que tuvo a los ángeles en
movimiento constante. La música en tubos
arriba del altar hacía como si la pequeña flauta
y el violín de los ángeles estuvieran producién-
dola. Como dice Chepa, "Hubo muchos cuellos
torcidos de estar mirando hacia arriba tanto
tiempo." El 6 de enero, los Tres Reyes Magos
se unieron al altar. Todas las figuras están
talladas del nervio del cactos saguaro; algunas
de las figuras están coyunturadas en la cintura
para inclinarse con reverencia. Misión de
San José, Pisinemo, Arizona.

58

the carving and the final touches. When she needs a ramada, her grandson Nicholas makes it for her. The Francos had four children, and both of their sons carry on the artistic tradition started by Domingo. Patrick has done some scenes in the past; their younger son Thomas continues to do them, as well as Nativity scenes, following the style of his parents.

Though it was difficult to start a new craft late in life, Chepa is proud that her Nativities and Papago scenes are now in collections throughout this country, as well as Germany, Denmark, Australia, and China. One of her Nativities has a special place of honor. It is in a cave called "The Children's Cave" or "Cave of Toys" in the Baboquivari Mountains south of Topowa, Arizona. Every Christmas it is lit with candles; Papagos from all over the reservation and visitors from other parts of the world make a pilgrimage there to view it.

mir." Jetzt macht sie sowohl die Schnitzarbeiten als auch die Ausschmückung. Wenn sie eine Ramada braucht, baut ihr Enkelkind Nicholas. Die Francos hatten vier Kinder, von denen die beiden Söhne die von Domingo begonnene künstlerische Tradition fortsetzen. Patrick schnitzte schon früher einige Szenen, und der jüngere Sohn Thomas führt das Werk fort und macht auch Weihnachtskrippen im Stil seiner Eltern.

Obwohl es schwierig war, in ihrem Alter ein neues Kunsthandwerk zu beginnen, ist Chepa stolz darauf, daß ihre Weihnachtskrippen und Papagoszenen sich jetzt in Sammlungen sowohl in den Vereinigten Staaten als auch in Deutschland, Dänemark, Australien und China befinden. Einer ihrer Weihnachtskrippen wird eine besondere Ehre zu Teil: sie steht im Baboquivari-Gebirge südlich von Topowa, Arizona, in einer Höhle, die als "Kinderhöhle" oder "Höhle der Spielzeuge" bezeichnet wird. Jedes Jahr zu Weihnachten wird sie mit Kerzen beleuchtet; die Papago-Indianer aus dem ganzen Reservat und Besucher aus aller Welt pilgern dorthin, um sie zu betrachten.

toques. Cuando necesita una ramada, su nieto Nicolás la hace para ella. Los Franco tienen cuatro hijos, y los dos muchachos siguen en la tradición artística que fundó Domingo. Patrick ha hecho algunas escenas en el pasado; Tomás, el hijo menor, los sigue haciendo, así como también los Nacimientos al estilo de sus padres.

Aunque fue difícil aprender un arte nuevo a una edad avanzada, Chepa está orgullosa de sus Nacimientos y escenas de los Pápagos que se encuentran en colecciones por los Estados Unidos así como también en Alemania, Dinamarca, Australia, y China. Un Nacimiento de ella ocupa un sitio de honor en una caverna llamada "La Caverna de los Niños" o "La Caverna de Juguetes" en las Montañas Baboquívari al sur de Topowa en Arizona. Cada año, en la Navidad, lo iluminan con velas. Los Indios Pápagos vienen de todas partes de la Reservación y visitantes de todo el mundo vienen en peregrinación para verlo.

ALFRED AGUILAR works in almost every art medium and has won awards in all of them at major southwestern shows. He made his first Nativity set in 1975. Although he has only done a few since, his treatment of the theme is unusual and appealing. One of his earliest sets, which he sold to a collector from Sweden, features a painted backdrop of the stable, mountain, and stars. He likes to do a different background treatment for each set.

He operates his own gallery and shop in San Ildefonso. So prodigious is his production that most of the items for sale there are his own creations — paintings, silk screen prints, pottery bowls and figures, and jewelry. Most of these are signed with his Indian name, Sa Wa Pin, meaning "High Sandstone Peaks." Often he will use both names to sign his poetry, which is printed on the cards he designs. One of his poems, "The Pottery," begins, "When clay sings I sing," and goes on to express the close kinship he feels for the clay. His paintings are in the permanent collection of the Museum of New Mexico, and one of his Storytellers is in the Smithsonian collection. He is particularly noted for his blackware buffalos, which

ALFRED AGUILAR übt fast jede Art von Kunsthandwerk aus und hat in führenden Ausstellungen des Südwestens Preise auf allen Gebieten erworben. Er schuf seine erste Weihnachtskrippe im Jahre 1975. Obwohl er seitdem nur wenige angefertigt hat, ist seine Behandlung dieses Themas ungewöhnlich und anziehend. Eine seiner frühesten Gruppen, die er einem Sammler aus Schweden verkauft hat, zeigt einen mit Stall, Bergen und Sternen bemalten Hintergrund, und er liebt es, den Hintergrund für jede Gruppe unterschiedlich zu gestalten.

Er hat seine eigene Galerie mit Verkaufsladen in San Ildefonso. Seine Produktivität ist derart groß, daß die meisten seiner Verkaufsgegenstände eigene Schöpfungen sind — Gemälde, Siebdrucke, Schalen und Gestalten aus Ton und Schmuck. Er signiert die meisten Objekte mit seinem indianischen Namen Sa Wa Pin, der "Hohe Sandsteingipfel" bedeutet. Oft signiert er seine Gedichte, die auf von ihm entworfene Kunstkarten gedruckt werden, mit seinen beiden Namen. Eines dieser Gedichte, das "Die Töpferkunst" heißt, fängt mit folgenden Worten an: "Wenn der Ton singt, singe auch ich", und der darauffolgende Text drückt sein Gefühl enger Verwandtschaft mit dem Ton aus. Seine Gemälde hängen in der Dauerausstellung des Museums von New Mexico, und eine seiner Erzählerfiguren befindet sich in der Kunstsammlung der Smithsonian Institution. Er ist vor allem wegen seiner Büffel in schwarzem Ton bekannt, die von

ALFRED AGUILAR trabaja en casi todos los medios artísticos y en todos ellos ha ganado premios en las exposiciones principales del Suroeste. Hizo su primer Nacimiento en 1975. Aunque sólo ha hecho unos pocos desde entonces, su enfoque del tema es único y atractivo. Una de sus primeros juegos, que vendió a un coleccionista sueco, destaca un telón pintado con establo, montañas, y estrellas. Le gusta crear un fondo diferente para cada colección.

Alfred dirige su propia galería y tienda en San Ildefonso. Su obra es tan prolífera que la mayor parte de los artículos que allí se encuentran a la venta son producto de su propia creación: pinturas, estampas en seda, vasijas y figuras de cerámica, y joyería. La mayor parte de ellas llevan su nombre indio, "Sa Wa Pin," que significa "Atlas Cumbres de Arenisca." A menudo usa los dos nombres para firmar su poesía, que aparece en las tarjetas que él diseña. Uno de sus poemas, "La Cerámica," comienza así: "Cuando la arcilla canta, yo canto," y continua a expresar la relación íntima que siente por la arcilla. Sus pinturas forman parte de la colección permanente del Museo de Nuevo México, y uno de sus Narradores de Cuentos se encuentra en la Colección Smithsonian. Se le conoce especialmente por sus búfalos de cerámica negra, que

ALFRED AGUILAR   8-piece set
   1″ to 5″ high   1976
Added to the eight human figures are gifts of
a drum, two tiny animal fetishes, and three
miniature pots. For background, the artist has
made two unbaked adobe brick forms in which
he has placed branches of dried leaves.
Distinctive features are the delicate variety of
colors and textures: the human figures are
painted before firing and left unpolished, while
the cradle and tiny gifts are polished. A Deer
Dancer and an Antelope Dancer, far right,
come to see the Infant Christ, and two
Wise Men bring gifts of a traditional Indian
wedding shawl and pottery. Artist's Collection,
San Ildefonso Pueblo, New Mexico.

ALFRED AGUILAR   Gruppe von acht
   Figuren   2,5 bis 15,7 cm hoch   1976
Neben den acht Menschenfiguren sind eine
Trommel, zwei kleine Tierfetische und drei
Miniaturtöpfe als Geschenke zu sehen.
Den Hintergrund hat der Künstler aus zwei
Lehmziegelformen gebildet, in die er
Zweige mit getrockneten Blättern gelegt hat.
Die delikate Verwendung der Farben und
die Behandlung der Tonoberflächen sind
charakteristische Merkmale: die Menschen-
gestalten werden vor dem Brennen bemalt und
unpoliert gelassen, während die Wiege und
die winzigen Geschenke poliert werden. Ein
Hirschtänzer und ein Antilopentänzer (weit
links) kommen, das Christkind anzuschauen, und
zwei Weise bringen einen traditionellen
indianischen Hochzeitsschal und Töpferwaren
als Geschenke. Sammlung des Künstlers,
San Ildefonso Pueblo, New Mexico.

ALFRED AGUILAR   juego de 8 piezas
   de 2.5 cm. a 15.7 cm. de alto   1976
Además de las ocho figuras humanas hay
regalos de un tambor, dos pequeñísimos
fetiches de animales, y tres ollitas en miniatura.
De fondo, el artista ha creado dos formas de
ladrillos de adobe sin cocer en las cuales ha
colocado ramas con hojas secas. Características
que sobresalen son la delicada variedad de
colores y las texturas: las figuras humanas están
pintadas antes de cocerlas al fuego y se las
deja sin pulir, en cambio la cuna y los pequeñísimos regalos están pulidos. Un bailarín de la
Danza del Venado y otro de la Danza del
Antílope, al fondo a la derecha, vienen a ver al
Cristo Infante, y dos Reyes Magos traen regalos
de una manta tradicional india de bodas, y
cerámica. De la colección del artista, el Pueblo
San Ildefonso, Nuevo México.

62

range from miniatures to ten inches high. In 1974 the Heard Museum's Sculpture II show included five of his ceramic figures.

Though he learned pottery making from his parents, Rosalie and Jose A. Aguilar, he is a self-taught painter. He was born in San Ildefonso on July 1, 1933, and attended Santa Fe Indian School and Pojoaque High School. During the Korean War, he served in the United States Air Force, stationed in France and Germany. He married Annabell Paisano of Laguna Pueblo; she and their six children are active in the arts, too, and several have won major awards. Aguilar notes: "The whole family takes part in the ceremonial dances. We have Deer Dances at Christmas and have the Matachine Dance, too. At San Ildefonso Catholic Church we do not have the other Nativity figures, but at Christmas Eve Mass the Baby Jesus is placed in a cradle next to the altar."

Miniaturen bis zu circa 25 cm hohen Figuren variieren. Im Jahre 1974 hat das Heard Museum fünf seiner Tonfiguren in seiner Skulpturausstellung II gezeigt.

Er lernte die Töpferkunst von seinen Eltern Rosalie und Jose A. Aguilar, ist jedoch ein Autodidakt auf dem Gebiet der Malerei. Er wurde am 1. Juli 1933 in San Ildefonso geboren und besuchte die Santa Fe Indianer-Schule (Grundschule) und Pojoaque High School (höhere Schule). Während des koreanischen Krieges diente er in der amerikanischen Luftwaffe und war in Frankreich und Deutschland stationiert. Er heiratete Annabell Paisano, die aus Laguna Pueblo stammt. Sie und ihre sechs Kinder sind auch künstlerisch tätig und haben viele Preise erworben. Aguilar bemerkt: "Die ganze Familie nimmt an den zeremoniellen Tänzen teil. Zu Weihnachten veranstalten wir Hirschtänze und auch den Matachine-Tanz. In der katholischen Kirche von San Ildefonso haben wir keine Gruppen von Weihnachtsfiguren, aber zur Weihnachtsmesse liegt das Christkind in einer Wiege neben dem Altar."

varían de tamaño desde miniaturas hasta los de veinte y cinco centímetros de alto. En 1974, la Exposición de Escultura II en el Museo Heard incluyó cinco de sus figuras de cerámica.

Aunque aprendió el arte de la cerámica de sus padres, Rosalie y José A. Aguilar, es un pintor autodidacta. Nació en San Ildefonso el 1 de julio de 1933 y asistió a la Escuela India de Santa Fe y a la Escuela Secundaria de Pojoaque. Durante la Guerra de Corea, servió en la Fuerza Aérea de los Estados Unidos, permaneciendo en Francia y Alemania. Se casó con Annabelle Paisano, del pueblo Laguna. Ella y sus seis hijos también participan en las actividades artísticas, y varios han recibido premios importantes. Aguilar señala: "Todo la familia participa de las danzas ceremoniales. Tenemos la Danza del Venado en Navidad y la Danza de Matachine también. En la Iglesia Católica de San Ildefonso no tenemos las otras figuras del Nacimiento, pero en la Misa de Gallo en Noche Buena, colocamos al Niño Jesús en una cuna al lado del altar."

SAN JUAN PUEBLO

REYCITA GARCIA'S Nativity sets reflect traditional San Juan pottery in the texturing and rich coloring of the red, tan, and white clays. Her close attention to costume detail also reflects her pueblo, which has become noted for its production of fashionable garments, weaving, and embroidery designs. Another distinctive feature of her work is the striking modeling of faces. Her adult male figures, with their white hair, jutting chins, and pursed-in lips suggesting toothlessness, have faces on which age has etched the lines of great character and are unlike any others to be found in southwest Indian Nativity interpretations. She began making Nacimientos around 1967. Just prior to that she had started doing small pottery and then small clay figures performing typical pueblo tasks, such as grinding corn. "One day," she says, "I was looking through a magazine and saw a Nativity set and I thought 'someday soon I'm going to try this.'" Not long after, she did try it and found that the figures she had already been modeling led quite naturally to Nativity figures.

She was born in San Juan on January 4, 1931. Her mother, Geronima Archulata, was a potter and taught the traditional techniques to her. Though Reycita never enters competitions now,

REYCITA GARCIAs Weihnachtskrippen spiegeln in der Beschaffenheit und reichen Färbung der roten, gelbbraunen und weißen Töne die traditionelle Keramik von San Juan wider. Auch die sorgsam ausgearbeiteten Details der Kostüme lassen den Einfluß ihres Pueblos erkennen, das durch seine modischen Gewänder und seine Weberei und Stickerei berühmt geworden ist. Ein weiteres Kennzeichen ihrer Arbeit ist die auffallende Modellierung der Gesichter. Ihre Männerfiguren, mit ihren weißen Haaren, vorspringendem Kinn und zusammengezogenen, Zahnlosigkeit andeutenden Lippen, zeigen Gesichter, in die das Alter die Züge charaktervoller Persönlichkeit eingeätzt hat; unter den südwestindianischen Krippenfiguren sind sie einmalig. Um 1967 herum fing sie an, Weihnachtskrippen zu gestalten, nachdem sie erst kurz vorher begonnen hatte, kleine Töpfe und dann kleine Tonfiguren anzufertigen, die typische Pueblo Arbeiten verrichten, wie das Mahlen von Mais. "Eines Tages," sagt sie, "blätterte ich in einer Zeitschrift, und als ich eine Weihnachtskrippe sah, dachte ich: 'Bald werde auch ich versuchen, eine Krippe zu machen.'" Nicht lange danach führte sie diese Idee aus, wobei sie entdeckte, daß die Figuren, die sie schon vorher modelliert hatte, sich ganz natürlich für Weihnachtskrippen eigneten.

Reycita wurde am 4. Januar 1931 geboren. Ihre Mutter, Geronima Archulata, war Töpferin und brachte ihr die traditionelle Arbeitstechnik bei. Obwohl Reycita heute nicht mehr an

Los Nacimientos de **REYCITA GARCIA** reflejan, en la textura y el rico colorido de las arcillas — roja, bronceada, y blanca — la cerámica tradicional de San Juan. La atención que pone a los detalles de la ropa también refleja aspectos de su pueblo que es conocido por la producción de vestidos de moda, tejidos, y diseños de bordados. Otra característica sobresaliente de su obra lo constituyen los impresionantes modelados de rostros. Las figuras de hombres de cabello blanco, barbillas salientes, y labios apretados que sugieren la falta de dientes, tienen rostros en los cuales el tiempo ha grabado señales de gran carácter, y no se parecen a nada de lo que se encuentra en las interpretaciones de Nacimientos del Suroeste. Comenzó creando Nacimientos aproximadamente en 1967. Anteriormente había comenzado a crear pequeñas piezas de cerámica y luego pequeñas figuras de arcilla realizando tareas típicas del pueblo, como por ejemplo moliendo maíz. "Un día," nos dice, "estaba mirando una revista cuando vi un Nacimiento y pensé: algún día, pronto, trataré de crear uno." Así lo hizo poco después y se dio cuenta que las figuras que había modelado antes se convirtieron fácilmente en figuras de Nacimientos.

Nació en San Juan, el 4 de enero de 1931. Gerónima Archulata, su madre, fue ceramista también y le enseñó la técnica tradicional. Aunque ahora Reycita no

REYCITA GARCIA 9-piece set
  3¼″ to 5″ high   ca. 1971
The white hair of Joseph and the three shepherds is a distinctive feature of this artist's Nativities, as are the contemporary clothes. Their cowboy-style shirts and Levi pants are precisely detailed with collars, buttons, and pockets — the pants have slit pockets in front and patch pockets in back. Each wears a belt with a different design. The Baby Jesus wears the perennially popular baby pajamas — Doctor Dentons — with five red buttons. In contrast to the men, Mary wears a simple white shift. The only polished surfaces are Mary's hair and the top of the metate cradle. Katherine H. Rust Children's Collection, Albuquerque, New Mexico.

REYCITA GARCIA   Gruppe von neun
  Figuren 8,3 bis 12,7 cm hoch   ca. 1971
Sowohl die weißen Haare Josephs und der drei Hirten wie auch die zeitgenössische Kleidung kennzeichnen die einzigartigen Weihnachtskrippen dieser Künstlerin. Ihre *Levi*-Hosen und Hemden im Cowboy-Stil werden mit Halskragen, Knöpfen und Taschen bis ins kleinste Detail modelliert — die vorderen Hosentaschen sind geschlitzt, die hinteren aufgesetzt. Jeder trägt einen Gürtel mit einem besonderen Muster. Das Christkind trägt die immer beliebten Baby-Pyjamas — Doctor Dentons — mit fünf roten Knöpfen. Im Gegensatz zu den Männern trägt Maria ein einfaches, weißes Kleid. Die einzigen polierten Flächen sind die Haare Marias und der obere Teil der *metate*-Wiege. Katherine H. Rust Kinderkunstsammlung, Albuquerque, New Mexico.

REYCITA GARCIA   juego de 9 piezas
  de 8.3 cm. a 12.7 cm. de alto   circa 1971
Características sobresalientes de los Nacimientos de esta artista son el cabello blanco de José y de los tres pastores, así como la vestimenta contemporánea. Sus camisas en el estilo vaquero y pantalones "Levi" han sido cuidadosamente detallados con cuellos, botones, bolsillos — los pantalones tienen bolsillos internos en el frente y bolsillos sobrepuestos atrás. Cada uno lleva un cinto con un diseño diferente. El Niño Jesús viste el tradicional pijama de bebé — "Doctor Dentons" — con cinco botones rojos. Contrastando con los hombres, María viste una túnica blanca y sencilla. Solamente el cabello de María y la parte superior de la cuna de metate han sido pulidos. De la Colección Infantil de Katherine H. Rust, Albuquerque, Nuevo México.

she took prizes in pottery while still attending San Juan Day School and periodically teaches the craft there. In 1950 she married Peter Garcia and began their family of nine children — five girls and four boys. All of her daughters make pottery and small animals and her son, Gordon, was making pottery before he was seven. Both she and her husband are active in San Juan Catholic Church and sing in the choir.

"At our church," she says, "the Nativity is set up next to the altar three or four days before Christmas and left there till after Kings' Day on January 6. In the last few years a special Christmas Eve Mass is read in Tewa, the language of our pueblo." She adds that she likes making Nativities. Inspiration is provided by the many pictures on her living room walls of the Madonna and Christ Child.

Kunstwettbewerben teilnimmt, hat sie schon während der Schulzeit in San Juan Auszeichnungen für ihre Töpferkunst erworben, und von Zeit zu Zeit gibt sie dort Keramikunterricht. Im Jahre 1950 sie Peter Garcia heiratete, und inzwischen hat sie ihm neun Kinder geboren — fünf Mädchen und vier Jungen. Die Töchter stellen alle Töpfe und kleine Tiere her, und ihr Sohn Gordon machte bereits Töpfe, bevor er sieben Jahre alt war. Sowohl Reycita als auch ihr Mann sind aktive Mitglieder der katholischen Kirche in San Juan und singen im Kirchenchor.

"In unserer Kirche," sagt sie, "wird die Weihnachtskrippe drei oder vier Tage vor Weihnachten neben dem Altar aufgestellt, und sie bleibt dort bis nach dem Fest der Heiligen drei Könige am 6. Januar. Seit den letzten Jahren wird am Heiligen Abend eine besondere Weihnachtsmesse in *Tewa*, der Sprache unseres Pueblos, gelesen." Sie fügt hinzu, daβ die Arbeit an Weihnachtskrippen ihr groβe Freude macht und daβ sie von den vielen an den Wänden ihres Wohnzimmers hängenden Bildern der Madonna und des Christkindes inspiriert wird.

participa en concursos, ganó premios en cerámica mientras asistía a la Escuela Diurna de San Juan y de vez en cuando enseña la artesanía allí mismo. En 1950 se casó con Peter García y empezó su familia de nueve hijos — cinco hijas y cuatro hijos. Todas sus hijas hacen cerámica y pequeños animales, y su hijo Gordon creaba piezas de cerámica antes de cumplir siete años. Ella y su esposo participan en las actividades de la Iglesia Católica de San Juan y cantan en el coro.

"En nuestra iglesia, el Nacimiento está colocado junto al altar tres o cuatro días antes de la Navidad y permanece allí hasta después del Día de los Reyes, el 6 de enero. En los últimos años se celebra una Misa de Gallo en Noche Bueno en Tewa, la lengua de nuestro pueblo," dice ella, y luego agrega que le gusta hacer Nacimientos. Varias pinturas de la Virgen y el Niño Jesús, colocadas en las paredes de su sala, le sirven de inspiración.

DOROTHY GUTIERREZ may be found most days of the week sitting at her kitchen table fashioning small figures of people and animals. Spread on the table is a newspaper on which is placed a pot of water, a chunk of clay, several toothpicks, and a popsicle stick. These are her only tools other than her nimble fingers. Her husband Paul, who does the sanding and polishing of her pieces, has impeccable qualifications. He is the son of Luther Gutierrez and the nephew of Margaret, the famous brother-and-sister team of potters (see page 70). From early childhood he helped polish the pottery of his grandmother, Lela Gutierrez, another well-known potter. When Dorothy first began making her clay figures in 1971, she had expert instruction from Margaret. During her first year Dorothy made ten Nativity sets, along with many miniature buffalos, beavers, bears, and wedding vases. Since 1972 when she began entering her work in competitions, she has been winning awards at all the major shows in the Southwest. In 1975 her seventeen-piece blackware Nativity won First Prize in sculpture at the fall Indian crafts show at the Deer Dancer Gallery in Denver. At the 1976 show, one of her miniature redware Nativities took Best of Show in the contemporary category, and she

DOROTHY GUTIERREZ findet man an den meisten Wochentagen an ihrem Küchentisch, wo sie kleine Menschen- und Tierfiguren aus Ton gestaltet. Auf einer auf dem Tisch ausgebreiteten Zeitung befinden sich ein Topf Wasser, ein Stück Ton, mehrere Zahnstocher und ein Ice-cream-Stäbchen. Dies sind außer ihren flinken Fingern ihre einzigen Werkzeuge. Ihr Mann Paul, der ihre Figuren mit Sand abreibt und poliert, hat einwandfreie Qualifikationen. Er ist der Sohn von Luther Gutierrez und der Neffe von Margaret, den berühmten Geschwistern, die zusammen das Töpferhandwerk ausüben. Von Kindheit an hat er seiner Großmutter Lela Gutierrez, einer bekannten Töpferin, beim Polieren ihrer Töpfe geholfen. Als Dorothy 1971 anfing, Tonfiguren zu machen, erhielt sie eine fachgerechte Ausbildung von Margaret. Im ersten Jahr schuf Dorothy zehn Weihnachtskrippen nebst vielen Miniaturen von Büffeln, Bibern und Bären und Hochzeitsvasen.

Seit sie 1972 an Wettbewerben teilzunehmen begann, hat sie Preise in allen größeren Ausstellungen des Südwestens erworben. Im Herbst 1975 hat sie mit ihrer aus siebzehn Figuren bestehenden Weihnachtskrippe aus schwarzem Ton in einer Ausstellung indianischer Handarbeit im *Deer Dancer* (einer Kunstgalerie in Denver, Colorado) den ersten Skulpturpreis erworben. Im Jahre 1976 hat sie mit einer Miniaturweihnachtskrippe aus rotem Ton wieder den ersten Preis für zeitgenössisches Kunsthandwerk

Casi todos los días de la semana, se puede encontrar a **DOROTHY GUTIERREZ** sentada a la mesa de su cocina modelando pequeñas figurillas de personas y animales. Encima de la mesa hay un periódico, un jarrito de agua, un pedazo de barro, varios palillos de dientes, y un palito. Estos son sus únicos instrumentos además de sus dedos ágiles. Su esposo Paul, que lija y pule las piezas, tiene cualificaciones impecables. Es el hijo de Luther Gutiérrez y el sobrino de Margaret Gutiérrez, el famoso equipo de hermanos ceramistas (ve pagina 70). Desde niño, ayudaba a pulir las piezas de cerámica de su abuela Lela Gutiérrez, otra ceramista famosa. Cuando Dorothy empezó a hacer sus figurillas de arcilla en 1971, recibió instrucción experta de Margaret. Durante el primer año, Dorothy hizo diez Nacimientos y, además, hizo búfalos, castores, y osos en miniatura, y floreros de boda. Desde que empezó a exhibir sus piezas en concursos en 1972, ha ganado premios en los más importantes del Suroeste. En 1975, recibió por su Nacimiento de 17 piezas en arcilla negra el primer premio de escultura en una exhibición de otoño de arte India en la galería Deer Dancer, Denver, Colorado. En 1976, uno de sus Nacimientos en miniatura de arcilla colorada recibió el Premio al Mejor en la categoría de

DOROTHY GUTIERREZ   13-piece set
   1¼″ to 4¼″ high   1977
Though the artist makes the majority of her
Nativities in the polished blackware for which
Santa Clara is noted, she has done several
sets in red and buff, both in the large size
shown here and in her miniatures. The buff, or
"white slip" as she calls it, is left unpolished
to create a rich contrast with the polished red
slip. The Three Wise Men bear gifts of a
redware jar, a wedding vase (with the double
spout), and an ear of corn. The shepherd
carries a reed staff and the Infant Jesus is
placed in a Navajo cradleboard, just 1¼ inches
high. Museum of Northern Arizona Shop,
Flagstaff, Arizona.

DOROTHY GUTIERREZ   Gruppe von
   dreizehn Figuren   3,2 bis 10,8 cm   1977
Obwohl die Künstlerin die Mehrzahl ihrer
Weihnachtskrippen aus dem berühmten
schwarzen Ton von Santa Clara gestaltet, hat
sie auch mehrere Gruppen in Rot und Hell-
braun geschaffen, sowohl größere Figuren, wie
hier abgebildet, als auch Miniaturen. Die
hellbraunen Oberflächen (*white slip*, wie sie es
nennt), werden unpoliert gelassen, um einen
starken Kontrast mit den polierten roten
(*red slip*) zu erzeugen. Die drei Weisen tragen
als Geschenke einen Topf aus rotem Ton, eine
Hochzeitsvase (mit doppeltem Ausguss) und
einen Maiskolben. Der Hirte trägt einen
Rohrstab, und das Christkind liegt in einer
typischen Navajo-Wiege, deren Höhe nur
3,2 cm beträgt. Verkaufsstelle des Museums
von Northern Arizona, Flagstaff, Arizona.

DOROTHY GUTIERREZ   juego de 13 piezas
   de 3.2 cm. a 10.8 cm. de alto   1977
Aunque la artista ha creado la mayor parte de
sus Nacimientos de arcilla negra pulida, por lo
que Santa Clara es reconocida, también ha
hecho varios juegos en cerámica colorada y
color piel de tamaños grandes y en miniatura.
La de color piel o "sellador blanco," como la
llama ella, se deja sin pulir para que haga un
rico contraste con el sellador colorado pulido.
Los Tres Reyes Magos llevan de regalo un
jarrito de arcilla colorada, un florero de bodas
(de dos picos), y una mazorca de maíz. El
pastor lleva un bastón de caña, y el Niño Jesús
está acostado sobre una cuna portátil Navajo,
de solo 3.2 centímetros de alto. Tienda del
Museo del Norte de Arizona, Flagstaff, Arizona.

has won the top awards every year since. In late 1976 she began making miniature Mudhead figures and included three of these in one of her blackware Nativities. She also has been making miniature turtles in red- and blackware and stringing them on necklaces.

Dorothy's maiden name was Pinto. She is of Navajo descent and was born in Gallup, New Mexico, on September 17, 1940. Though she had no early training in pottery making, her mother was an expert weaver and she was exposed to the traditional Navajo crafts. After attending Torreon Day School on the reservation, she went to Haskell Institute at Lawrence, Kansas, and then the Indian School at Albuquerque. She and Paul and their two sons attend Santa Clara Catholic Church. Paul also takes part in the pueblo's Indian ceremonials.

gewonnen, und seitdem hat sie jedes Jahr wichtige Preise erhalten. Gegen Ende des Jahres 1976 hat sie angefangen, kleine *Mudhead*-Figuren (Spassmacher bei den Pueblo-Tänzen) zu produzieren; drei davon hat sie einer ihrer Weihnachtskrippen in schwarzem Ton beigegeben. Sie modelliert auch Miniaturschildkröten in rotem und schwarzem Ton und reiht sie dann auf Halsketten auf.

Dorothys Familienname war Pinto. Sie kommt aus dem Navajo-Stamm und wurde am 17. September 1940 in Gallup, New Mexico, geboren. Zwar erhielt sie keine frühe Ausbildung in der Töpferkunst, aber ihre Mutter war eine hervorragende Weberin, und von ihr lernte Dorothy die traditionellen Navajo-Handwerkskünste kennen. Nachdem sie zur Torreon-Tagesschule im Reservat ging, studierte sie am Haskell Institut in Lawrence, Kansas, und dann an der Indianer-Schule in Albuquerque, New Mexico. Sie, ihr Mann Paul und ihre zwei Söhne sind Mitglieder der katholischen Kirche in Santa Clara. Paul nimmt auch an den indianischen Zeremonien seines Pueblos teil.

contemporáneos, y desde entonces ha recibido los primeros premios cada año. A fines de 1976, empezó a hacer "Mudhead" figuras en miniatura e incluyó tres de ellas en un Nacimiento de arcilla negra. También ha hecho tortugas de arcilla roja y negra en miniatura, y enzartándolas en collares.

El apellido de soltera de Dorothy fue Pinto. Nació en Gallup, Nuevo México, el 17 de septiembre de 1940, de descendencia Navajo. Aunque nunca tuvo un temprano entrenamiento en la hechura de cerámica, su madre era una tejedora experta y fue expuesta a la artesanía de los Navajos. Después de haber asistido a la Escuela Diurna Torreón en la Reservación, asistió al Instituto Haskell en Lawrence, Kansas, y después, a la Escuela India en Albuquerque. Ella y Paul y sus dos hijos asisten a la Iglesia Católica de Santa Clara. Paul también participa en los ceremoniales indios del pueblo.

MARGARET and LUTHER
GUTIERREZ, a sister-and-brother team,
are newcomers to the Nativities field,
having just begun making them in
1978. But they have long been noted in
the pottery field and are widely
known as simply "Margaret and Luther."
Theirs is a distinguished heritage:
"Our pottery has come down to us
through four generations, beginning with
our great-great-grandfather." Both of
their parents, Lela and Van, were out-
standing potters and worked as a team
for fifty years' until Van's death in 1956.
Then the mother and son, Lela and
Luther, worked as a team, producing
many notable pieces until her death
in 1966.

"After my mother passed away,"
Margaret notes, "I took over, and Luther
and I have been working together ever
since." Both were born in Santa Clara
Pueblo: Luther, on December 12, 1911,
and Margaret, on December 16, 1936.
Margaret began making little animals of
clay when she was five years old and
continues to do the modeling for their
pieces, while Luther does the painted
decoration. They have won many
awards for their pottery vessels and
animals; their work is in many
permanent collections, including the
Smithsonian Institution of Washington,
D.C., the Heard Museum, Phoenix, and
the Museum of New Mexico. Some
of their work is featured in a gallery in
Zurich, Switzerland. In 1972 they

MARGARET und LUTHER
GUTIERREZ, ein Geschwisterpaar,
sind Neulinge auf dem Gebiet der Weihnachtskrippen, da sie erst 1978 angefangen haben, solche gemeinsam anzufertigen. Sie sind jedoch schon lange als
Töpfer bekannt und werden weit und
breit einfach "Margaret und Luther"
genannt. Sie stammen aus einer bemerk-
enswerten Familie: "Von unserem
Ururgroßvater her wurde uns die Töpferkunst durch vier Generationen über-
liefert." Ihre beiden Eltern, Lela und
Van, waren hervorragende Töpfer und
arbeiteten fünfzig Jahre lang zusammen,
bis der Vater 1956 verstarb. Dann
arbeiteten Mutter und Sohn, Lela und
Luther, zusammen und schufen viele
bemerkenswerte Stücke, bis auch sie
1966 verschied.

"Nach dem Tod meiner Mutter,"
erklärt Margaret, "nahm ich ihre Stelle
ein; seitdem arbeiten Luther und ich
zusammen." Die beiden wurden im
Santa Clara Pueblo geboren: Luther
am 12. Dezember 1911 und Margaret
am 16. Dezember 1936. Margaret fing
schon mit fünf Jahren an, kleine Tiere
aus Ton zu gestalten, und sie fährt fort,
ihre gemeinsamen Figuren zu modellieren, während Luther sie bemalt.
Für ihre Tongefäße und -tiere haben
sie viele Preise erhalten, und man
findet ihre Kunsterzeugnisse in vielen
Dauerausstellungen, zum Beispiel in der
Smithsonian Institution in Washington,
D.C., dem Heard Museum in Phoenix
und im Museum von New Mexico.
Einige ihrer Werke befinden sich in einer
Kunstgalerie in Zürich. Im Jahre 1972

Los hermanos MARGARET y LUTHER
GUTIERREZ son nuevos en el campo
de la creación de Nacimientos, habiendo
empezado a hacerlos en 1978. Sin
embargo, ya eran famosos como ceramistas y conocidos simplemente como
"Margaret y Luther." La de ellos es una
herencia distinguida: "Nuestra cerámica
viene de cuatro generaciones atrás,
empezando con nuestro tatarabuelo."
Sus padres, Lela y Van, fueron ceramistas excepcionales y trabajaron en con-
junto por cincuenta años hasta la muerte
de Van en 1956. Entonces, la madre y el
hijo, Lela y Luther, trabajaron juntos,
creando muchas piezas notables hasta la
muerte de Lela en 1966.

"Después de la muerte de mi madre,"
dice Margaret, "tomé su posición y
Luther y yo hemos trabajado juntos
desde entonces." Los dos nacieron en el
pueblo de Santa Clara: Luther, el 12 de
diciembre de 1911, y Margaret, el 16 de
diciembre de 1936. Cuando cumplió
cinco años, Margaret empezó a hacer
animalitos de arcilla; hoy en día continua
diseñando las piezas, y Luther pinta las
decoraciones. Los dos han ganado
muchos premios por sus vasijas y animales de cerámica; sus obras se encuentran en muchas colecciones permanentes,
incluyendo las del Instituto Smithsonian
en Washington, D.C., el Museo Heard
de Phoenix, y el Museo de Nuevo
México. Algunas se exhiben en una

MARGARET and LUTHER   10-piece set
   1½″ to 4″ high   1978
The animated expressions of both the human
and animal figures are a trademark of this
sister-and-brother team. Another trademark is
the highly polished buff clay, often with a
red slip, with detailing in red, black, and grey.
Margaret notes: "Besides the Holy Family,
our sets usually have the Three Wise Men,
three shepherds, and three animals." Here there
are just two wise men bearing pottery and a
single shepherd carrying two lambs, while
a cow, lamb, and two donkeys look on.
Museum of Northern Arizona Shop,
Flagstaff, Arizona.

MARGARET und LUTHER   Gruppe von
   zehn Figuren   3,8 bis 10,1 cm hoch   1978
Der lebendige Ausdruck sowohl der Menschen-
als auch der Tierfiguren kennzeichnet die
Arbeiten dieses Geschwisterpaars. Ein weiteres
Kennzeichen ist der hochpolierte gelbbraune
Ton, oft mit einem roten, geschlämmten
Überzug, mit detaillierter Bemalung in Rot,
Schwarz und Grau. Margaret erklärt: "Außer
der Heiligen Familie enthalten unsere Gruppen
gewöhnlich die drei Weisen, drei Hirten und
drei Tiere." Hier sieht man nur zwei Weisen,
die irdene Gefäße bringen, einen einzigen
Hirten, der zwei Lämmer trägt, und eine Kuh,
ein Lamm und zwei Esel, die ihnen zuschauen.
Verkaufsstelle des Museums von Northern
Arizona, Flagstaff, Arizona.

MARGARET Y LUTHER   juego de 10 piezas
   de 3.8 cm. a 10.1 cm. de alto   1978
Las expresiones animadas de ambas las figuras
humanas y los animales son una característica
exclusiva de las obras de estos hermanos. Otra
característica es la arcilla de color piel sumamente pulida, a menudo con un sellador colorado con detalles en rojo, negro, y gris.
Margaret observa: "Además de la Sagrada
Familia, nuestros juegos contienen usualmente
los Tres Reyes Magos, tres pastores, y tres
animales." Aquí, hay solamente dos Reyes
Magos trayendo cerámica y un solo pastor
cargando dos ovejas, mientras que una vaca,
una oveja, y dos burros observan. Tienda del
Museo del Norte de Arizona, Flagstaff, Arizona.

toured Europe for two months with a group of Indian artists, giving pottery demonstrations and lectures.

Their whimsical animal figures have always been popular, and the transition to making Nativities was an easy and natural one for them. Margaret notes, "We have had many requests for Nacimientos in the past and lately there has been more demand. One day last year I thought, 'I'm going to start something new,' and I made a Nacimiento. Since then we have made about twenty sets, usually of nine to twelve pieces. Some people ask for more animals or a stable and we will make them on special order. The stables are made of clay blocks with wood poles, vigas, and a tin roof."

gingen sie mit einer Gruppe indianischer Künstler auf eine zweimonatige Vortragsreise durch Europa, um ihre Technik des Töpferhandwerks vorzuführen.

Ihre lustigen Tierfiguren waren seit jeher beliebt, und der Übergang zur Produktion von Weihnachtskrippen war für die Künstler leicht und natürlich. Margaret erklärt: "Wir hatten schon vorher viele Bestellungen für *Nacimientos* und neuerdings hat die Nachfrage zugenommen. Im vergangenen Jahr dachte ich mir eines Tages: 'Ich werde etwas Neues anfangen', und ich schuf eine Weihnachtskrippe. Seitdem haben wir etwa zwanzig Gruppen angefertigt, die in der Regel aus neun bis zwölf Figuren bestehen. Manche Leute wünschen sich mehr Tiere oder einen Stall, und wir machen sie auf Sonderbestellung. Die Ställe werden aus Tonziegeln, Holzpfosten, Balken (*vigas*) und einem Blechdach gestaltet."

galería en Zurich, Suiza. En 1972 recorrieron Europa por dos meses con un grupo de artistas indios, y realizaron demostraciones y conferencias sobre la cerámica.

Sus figuras caprichosas de animales siempre han sido populares, y la transición a hacer los Nacimientos fue fácil y natural para ellos. Margaret observa: "Hemos tenido muchos pedidos de Nacimientos en el pasado, y recientemente la demanda ha aumentado. Un día, el año pasado, pensé, 'Voy a empezar algo nuevo,' e hice un Nacimiento. Desde entonces hemos hecho aproximadamente veinte juegos, usualmente de nueve a doce piezas. Algunas personas piden más animales o un establo, y se los hacemos por encargo especial. Los establos son hechos con bloques de arcilla con postes de madera, vigas, y un techo de hojalata."

MARIA I. NARANJO was the first potter in Santa Clara to make Nativities and the first among any of the pueblo artists to do them in blackware. She recalls: "I always admired the Italian Nativity at our Catholic church here, and in 1963 or 1964, I decided to make one for myself. I did it in the Spanish style with the figures in different colors." In 1965 when the Museum of New Mexico commissioned her to do a Nativity for the opening of their new shop, she began making blackware Spanish-style sets. "In 1969," she says, "I started doing Indian-style sets in black, and in 1973 I began doing some in redware." One redware set features the Wise Men in Plains Indian costumes, with braided hair and bearing gifts of a bow and arrow, beads, and a rattle. Recently she has been doing miniature sets in polished red, white, or black clay. An inventive and prolific artist, she has been noted for many years for her polished blackware *animalitos*. In these miniatures, she does every type of animal — from swans, skunks, and squirrels to dachshunds. Her larger animals — buffalos, elephants, horses, bears and goats — have the quality of fine sculpture and have won numerous awards. Among her human figures,

MARIA I. NARANJO war die erste Töpferin in Santa Clara, die Weihnachtskrippen anfertigte, und von allen Pueblo-Künstlerinnen die erste, die sie aus schwarzem Ton gestaltete. Sie erinnert sich: "Ich habe die italienische Weihnachtskrippe in unserer hiesigen katholischen Kirche immer bewundert, und im Jahre 1963 oder 1964 entschloβ ich mich, selbst eine solche Krippe zu machen. Ich gestaltete sie im spanischem Stil mit mehrfarbigen Figuren." Im Jahre 1965, als sie vom Museum von New Mexico beauftragt wurde, eine Weihnachtskrippe für die Eröffnung seiner neuen Verkaufsstelle zu schaffen, begann sie, Gruppen aus schwarzem Ton im "spanischen Stil" anzufertigen. "Im Jahre 1969," sagt sie, "habe ich angefangen, Gruppen im indianischen Stil in Schwarz, und seit 1973 auch in Rot zu machen." Eine der Gruppen in Rot stellt die drei Weisen in der Tracht der Prärieindianer dar, mit geflochtenem Haar, und mit Pfeil und Bogen, Perlen und einer Rassel als Geschenke. In letzter Zeit bildet sie Miniaturgruppen aus poliertem rotem, weiβem oder schwarzem Ton. Diese schöpferische und produktive Künstlerin ist schon seit Jahren wegen ihrer *animalitos* (Tierchen) aus schwarzem poliertem Ton bekannt. Unter diesen Miniaturen befinden sich alle möglichen Tierarten, beispielsweise Schwäne, Stinktiere, Eichhörnchen und Dackel. Ihre größeren Tiere — Büffel, Elefanten, Pferde, Bären, und Ziegen — sind von hervorragender plastischer Qualität und haben viele Preise erworben. Unter ihren

MARIA I. NARANJO fue la primera ceramista en Santa Clara en crear Nacimientos y fue la primera entre los artistas de los pueblos que las hizo de arcilla negra. Recuerda que: "Siempre admiraba el Nacimiento italiano en la Iglesia Católica aquí, y en 1963 o en 1964 decidí crear un Nacimiento para yo mismo. Lo hice al estilo español con figuras de varios colores." En 1965, cuando el Museo de Nuevo México le encargó que hiciera un Nacimiento para la apertura de la tienda nueva en el museo, comenzó a crear los juegos de arcilla negra al estilo español. Nos dice: "En 1969 comencé a crear juegos al estilo indio de arcilla negra y en 1973 de arcilla roja." Un juego de arcilla roja contiene los Tres Reyes Magos con el pelo trenzado, vestidos con los trajes de los Indios Plains y trayendo regalos de un arco y flecha, lentejuelas, y un sonajero. En los últimos años ha creado juegos en miniatura de cerámica roja, blanca, o negra. María es una artista imaginativa y fecunda; por muchos años ha sido reconocida por sus "animalitos" de arcilla negra, pulida. Entre estas miniaturas se encuentran toda clase de animales: desde cisnes, zorrillos, y ardillas, hasta perros "dachshund." Sus animales mayores (búfalos, elefantes, caballos, osos, y cabras) poseen la calidad de escultura fina y han ganado muchos premios. Entre sus figuras

MARIA I. NARANJO   9-piece set
  2″ to 5¼″ high   1973
Here Maria does the Nativity in polished
redware. Though the Holy Family and animals
are similar to those in her blackware sets,
the Three Wise Men are Plains Indian in
costume and hairstyles. In her home she pointed
to a photograph of her grandfather taken in
1898 by the Smithsonian Institution: "I try to
make my figurines look like him, with the
braided hair." The gifts they bring are also
Plains Indian — a string of beads, a rattle, and
bow and arrow. The clay cradle on legs
represents her second style; in later sets she
used the dish or metate style. Sallie R. Wagner,
Santa Fe, New Mexico.

MARIA I. NARANJO   Gruppe von neun
  Figuren   5,1 bis 13,3 cm hoch   1973
Hier fertigte Maria die Weihnachtskrippe in
poliertem rotem Ton an. Obwohl die Heilige
Familie und die Tiere denjenigen aus
schwarzem Ton ähneln, sind die drei Weisen
sowohl in der Kleidung als auch im Haarstil
als Prärieindianer dargestellt. In ihrem Haus
deutete sie auf ein Foto ihres Groβvaters, das
1898 von der Smithsonian Institution aufgenommen wurde: "Ich versuche, meinen
Figürchen sein Aussehen zu geben, insbesondere das geflochtene Haar." Die von den
Weisen gebrachten Geschenke sind ebenfalls
Gegenstände der Prärieindianer — eine
Perlenkette, eine Rassel, Pfeil und Bogen. Die
auf Beinen stehende Wiege aus Ton stammt
aus ihrer zweiten Stilperiode; in späteren
Gruppen fertigte sie den Schüssel- oder
Metate-Stil. Sallie R. Wagner, Santa Fe,
New Mexico.

MARIA I. NARANJO   juego de 9 piezas
  de 5.1 cm. a 13.3 cm. de alto   1973
Aquí María crea el Nacimiento en cerámica
roja pulida. Aunque la Sagrada Familia y los
animales son semejantes a los en sus juegos de
cerámica negra, los Tres Reyes Magos son
Indios Plains con vestidos y peinados típicos.
En su casa nos mostró una fotografía de su
abuelo que el Instituto Smithsonian sacó en
1898: "Trato que mis figuras se parezcan a él,
con el cabello trenzado." Los regalos que traen
también son objetos de los Indios Plains: una
cadena de lentejuelas, un sonajero, y un arco y
flecha. La cuna de arcilla sobre patas representa
su segundo estilo; en juegos más recientes usó
el estilo "metate." Sallie R. Wagner,
Santa Fe, Nuevo México.

74

MARIA I. NARANJO   9-piece set
    2½″ to 4½″ high   1965
This set was commissioned for the opening of
the Museum of New Mexico Shop in 1965 and
was the first Indian-made Nativity to be
exhibited there. A photograph of the set was
featured on Christmas cards sold in the shop
that year. For her early "Spanish-style" sets,
Maria says, she made the cradles in the
traditional way, with twigs interlaced on crossed
wooden legs, as shown here. Later, for her
"Indian-style" Nativities, she made clay cradles.
The three small animals in the foreground,
typical of the varied miniatures Maria creates,
were added by the collector to the six
original figures. Robert A. Ewing,
Santa Fe, New Mexico.

MARIA I. NARANJO   Gruppe von neun
    Figuren   6,4 bis 11,4 cm hoch   1965
Diese Gruppe wurde 1965 für die Eröffnung
der Verkaufsstelle des Museums von New
Mexico in Auftrag gegeben und war die erste
von einem Indianer geschaffene Weihnachtskrippe, die dort ausgestellt wurde. Die Gruppe
wurde auf Weihnachtskarten abgebildet, die
das Museum in jenem Jahr verkaufte. Von
ihren frühen Gruppen "im spanischen Stil"
sagt Maria, daβ sie die Wiegen auf traditionelle
Weise aus geflochtenen Zweigen und mit
gekreuzten Holzbeinen gestaltete, wie die
Abbildung zeigt. Später formte sie Wiegen aus
Ton für ihre Weihnachtskrippen "im indianischen Stil." Die drei kleinen Tiere im
Vordergrund, die typisch sind für die mannig-
faltigen Miniaturen Marias, hat der Sammler
den ursprünglich sechs Figuren hinzugefügt.
Robert A. Ewing, Santa Fe, New Mexico.

MARIA I. NARANJO   juego de 9 figuras
    de 6.4 cm. a 11.4 cm. de alto   1965
Este juego se lo encargaron para la inauguración de la Tienda del Museo de Nuevo México
en 1965 y fue el primer Nacimiento hecho por
un indio que se exhibió allí. Una fotografía de
este juego apareció en las tarjetas de Navidad
que se vendieron en la tienda ese año. María
dice que en sus primeros juegos del estilo
español creó las cunas al estilo tradicional, con
ramitas entrelazadas sobre las patas de madera
cruzadas, como se ve aquí. Luego construyó
cunas de cerámica para sus Nacimientos al
estilo indio. Los tres animalitos en el primer
plano son típicos de las varias miniaturas que
crea María. Fueron agregados por el coleccionista a las seis figuras originales. Robert A.
Ewing, Santa Fe, Nuevo México.

the most unusual for a pueblo artist is "The Flight into Egypt," Mary and the Infant Jesus on a donkey, done in 1975.

To early collectors she was known as "Margaret," but in recent years she has used her given name. She was born in Santa Clara on October 21, 1919. Her mother died when Maria was six. Under the care of her father, Abristo Naranjo, a well-known potter, she began making animal figures at the age of seven. Later she did the polishing and firing of his figurines. One of their pieces is in the permanent collection of the Museum of New Mexico. After schooling in the pueblo and in Santa Fe, she married Ignacio Naranjo, and they had three daughters.

Maria notes: "My daughter, Martha Mirabal, does miniature Nativities. Also, my granddaughter, Tammie Mirabal, age eight, has been doing unpolished Nativities and figurines since age four without any corrections from us."

Menschenfiguren ist die 1975 angefertigte "Flucht nach Ägypten" — Maria und das Christkind auf einem Esel — für eine Pueblo-Künstlerin die ungewöhnlichste.

Frühe Kunstsammler kannten sie als "Margaret", aber in letzter Zeit hat sie ihren Vornamen "Maria" benutzt. Sie wurde am 21. Oktober 1919 in Santa Clara geboren. Ihre Mutter starb als Maria erst sechs Jahre alt war. Unter der Aufsicht ihres Vaters Abristo Naranjo, der auch als Töpfer bekannt ist, fing sie mit sieben Jahren an, Tierfiguren zu gestalten, und später polierte und brannte sie seine Figürchen. Eine ihrer gemeinsam geschaffenen Figuren befindet sich in der Dauerausstellung des Museums von New Mexico. Nachdem sie im Santa Clara Pueblo und in Santa Fe zur Schule gegangen war, heiratete sie Ignacio Naranjo und gebar ihm drei Töchter. Maria bemerkt: "Meine Tochter Martha Mirabal gestaltet Miniaturweihnachtskrippen. Auch meine achtjährige Enkelin Tammie Mirabal macht schon seit vier Jahren — ohne irgendwelche Verbesserungen unsererseits — unpolierte Weihnachtskrippen und Figürchen."

humanas, la más raro para un artista de pueblo es "La huida a Egipto," María y el Niño Jesús en un burro, creada en 1975.

Los primeros coleccionistas la conocían como "Margaret," pero en los últimos años ha usado su nombre verdadero. Nació en Santa Clara el 21 de octubre en 1919. Su madre murió cuando María tenía seis años. Bajo la dirección de su padre, el famoso ceramista Abristo Naranjo, ella comenzó a crear figuras de animales cuando tenía siete años. Más tarde, ella pulía y cocía las figuras de él. Una de ellas está en la exhibición permanente en el Museo de Nuevo México. Después de acabar la escuela en el pueblo y en Santa Fe, se casó con Ignacio Naranjo. Los dos tuvieron tres hijas.

María observa: "Mi hija, Martha Mirabal, crea Nacimientos en miniatura. Mi nieta, Tammie Mirabal, de ocho años, también ha hecho Nacimientos sin pulir desde que tenía cuatro años y sin que tuviéramos que corregirla."

ALMA CONCHA says of her Naci-mientos: "It is my way of putting the Holy Family in homes. I hope people will see it and remember what Christmas is about. I hope, too, it will remind them that not all Christians are white, that they are of all nationalities." Around 1968, after seeing a Christmas show at the Picuris museum, she made her first Nativity set and has since become one of the most prolific artisans in the field. Her style is easily identified — clean-lined and sophisticated, and as one expert notes, "almost modern Danish in its simplicity." Her figures have no painted detailing — faces and clothes are delineated only with two slips of red and buff clay.

"When I first began making Naci-mientos," she notes, "I made only about three sets a year, just for Christmas shows; by 1976 I was making 100." She says that her three-piece sets of the Holy Family account for most of her production, fifty to seventy-five a year. In 1974 she began making ten- to thirteen-piece sets, adding the Three Wise Men and animals; in 1978 she added angels. Her miniature sets, which she started making in 1972, feature figures that are one-fourth to one and three-fourths inches

ALMA CONCHA sagt über ihre *Nacimientos*: "Auf diese Weise bringe ich die Heilige Familie den Leuten ins Haus. Ich hoffe, die Menschen werden sie sehen und sich auf die Bedeutung der Weihnachtsfeier besinnen. Sie wird sie dabei auch hoffentlich daran erinnern, daβ nicht alle Christen Weiβe sind, sondern daβ sie allen Nationalitäten angehören." Nachdem sie circa 1968 im Museum in Picuris eine Weihnachtsausstellung besichtigt hatte, machte sie ihre erste Weihnachtskrippe; sie ist seitdem zu einer der produktivsten Kunsthandwerkerinnen auf diesem Gebiet geworden. Ein Fachmann hat ihren hochentwickelten, an seinen klaren Linien leicht erkennbaren Stil als "fast modern-dänisch in seiner Schlichtheit" bezeichnet. Ihre Gestalten weisen keine detaillierte Bemalung auf, sondern Gesichter und Kleider werden einfach durch zwei Überzüge aus rotem und gelbbraunem Ton dargestellt.

"Als ich zum ersten Mal anfing, *Nacimientos* zu machen," sagt sie, "verfertigte ich nur etwa drei Gruppen im Jahr — nur für Weihnachtsausstellungen; 1976 produzierte ich schon hundert." Sie erklärt, daβ ihre Produktion zum gröβten Teil aus den Dreifigurengruppen der Heiligen Familie besteht, ungefähr fünfzig bis fünfundsiebzig im Jahr. Im Jahre 1974 fing sie an, Gruppen mit zehn bis dreizehn Figuren zu gestalten, wobei sie die drei Weisen und Tiere hinzufügte; 1978 fügte sie Engel hinzu. Ihre Miniaturgruppen, die sie seit 1972 herstellt, bestehen aus mit weichen Pastellfarben bemalten

Dice ALMA CONCHA de sus Nacimientos: "Es mi manera de poner la Sagrada Familia en los hogares. Espero que cuando la gente los vea se acuerden del significación de la Navidad. Espero, también, que les recuerde que no todos los Cristianos son blancos, sino que los hay de todas las razas y nacionalidades." Después de ver una exposición de Navidad en el Museo de Picuris aproximadamente en 1968, ella hizo su primer Nacimiento y, desde entonces, se ha convertido en una de las artesanas más prolíficas en su campo. Su estilo de líneas limpias y sofisticadas se identifica fácilmente. Un crítico nota que su estilo "es casi Danés moderno por su simplicidad." Sus figuras no poseen detalles pintados — las caras y la ropa están delineadas solamente con dos selladores de arcilla colorada y color piel.

"Cuando empecé a hacer Nacimientos," dice Alma, "Solamente hacía como tres juegos al año, especialmente para las exposiciones de Navidad; para 1976, ya hacía cien." Dice que sus juegos de tres piezas de la Sagrada Familia constituyen la mayor parte de su producción, de cincuenta a setenta y cinco juegos al año. En 1974, empezó a hacer juegos de diez a trece piezas, añadiendo los Tres Reyes Magos y animales; en 1978, agregó ángeles. En 1972, comenzó a hacer juegos en miniatura que se caracterizan por figuras de 0.6 a 4.4 centímetros de alto, pintadas de colores pastel

ALMA CONCHA   6-piece set
     2″ to 5¾″ high   1976
This Holy Family is typical of the artist's
popular three-piece sets. The Smithsonian
Institution purchased one of these in 1976 for
their permanent collection. If she adds animals,
they are usually a cow and two lambs as
shown here. She makes her figures in various
sizes ranging from miniatures to medium size
(about 4½ inches high) to large size (5¾ to 6
inches high). She achieves her unique effect
with just two slips of red and buff clay.
Originally she polished the red slip but now
does not except on special order.
Museum of New Mexico Shop,
Santa Fe, New Mexico.

ALMA CONCHA   Gruppe von sechs Figuren
     5 bis 14,6 cm hoch   1976
Diese Heilige Familie ist kennzeichnend für
die beliebten Dreifigurengruppen der
Künstlerin. Die Smithsonian Institution hat
1976 eine davon für ihre ständige Sammlung
gekauft. Wenn Alma Tiere hinzufügt, sind es
gewöhnlich eine Kuh und zwei Lämmer,
wie das Bild hier zeigt. Sie gestaltet ihre
Figuren in verschiedenen Größen — Miniaturen,
mittelgroß (etwa 11 cm hoch) und groß
(14,6 bis 15,2 cm hoch). Ihre einzigartige Wir-
kung erreicht sie mit nur zwei geschlämmten
Überzügen aus rotem und braungelbem Ton.
Ursprünglich hat sie den roten Überzug poliert;
jetzt wird er nur noch auf Bestellung poliert.
Verkaufsstelle des Museums von New Mexico,
Santa Fe, New Mexico.

ALMA CONCHA   juego de 6 piezas
     de 5 cm. a 14.6 cm. de alto   1976
Esta Sagrada Familia es típica de los populares
juegos de tres piezas de la artista. El Instituto
Smithsonian compró uno de éstos en 1976 para
su colección permanente. Si agrega animales,
generalmente aparecen una vaca y dos corderos,
como aquí. Alma hace figuras en varios
tamaños, desde miniaturas a tamaño mediano
(aproximadamente 11 centímetros de alto)
y grandes (de 14.6 a 15.2 centímetros de alto).
Consigue un efecto único con sólo dos selladores
de color rojo y color piel. Originalmente pulía
el sellador rojo, pero ahora no, excepto en
pedidos especiales. Tienda del Museo de
Nuevo México, Santa Fe.

ALMA CONCHA   11-piece set
   1″ to 5″ high   1978
Here she has added the Three Kings and their
tiny gifts of corn, bread, and chili, four animals,
and an angel. Her angels, in contrast to her
other figures, are decorated — finely detailed
designs are drawn on their wings and halos.
The Baby Jesus is depicted by a simple
egg shape placed in an Indian cradleboard.
Alma notes: "I used to show the men with their
hair in the Jemez chongo knot, but now I do
the braided style of Taos." The Taos-Pueblo-
style adobe stable was made by the collector.
Alexander E. Anthony, Jr.,
Albuquerque, New Mexico.

ALMA CONCHA   Gruppe von elf Figuren
   2,5 bis 12,5 cm hoch   1978
Die Künstlerin hat dieser Gruppe die drei
Könige mit winzigen Geschenken von Mais,
Brot und Pfefferfrüchten beigefügt, sowie
vier Tiere und einen Engel. Im Gegensatz zu
den andern Figuren sind Almas Engel fein
verziehrt, mit Mustern auf den Flügeln und
Heiligenscheinen. Das Christkind ist ein
einfaches, eiförmiges Figürchen in einer
Indianerwiege. Alma sagt: "Früher habe ich
die Männer mit dem *Chongo*-Haarknoten
von Jemez dargegestellt, aber jetzt zeige ich
sie im Taos-Stil mit Haarflechten." Der Stall
aus Ton im Taos-Stil wurde vom Sammler
angefertigt. Alexander E. Anthony, Jr.,
Albuquerque, New Mexico.

ALMA CONCHA   juego de 11 piezas
   de 5 cm. a 14.6 cm. de alto   1978
Aquí ha agregado los Tres Reyes Magos y los
pequeños regalos: maíz, pan, y chiles, cuatro
animales, y un ángel. Sus ángeles, en contraste
con sus otras figuras, son decorado — diseños
detallados son dibujados en las alas y las
aureolas. El Niño Jesús está representado por
una forma simple de huevo colocada en una
cuna portátil india. Alma dice: "Antes hacía a
los hombres con el pelo en moño al estilo
"chongo" de Jemez, pero ahora los hago con el
estilo trenzado de Taos." El establo hecho de
adobe al estilo del Taos Pueblo fue creado por
el coleccionista. Alexander E. Anthony, Jr.,
Albuquerque, Nuevo México.

high and painted in soft pastels, but recently she has made some in the red and buff, as she does for her larger sets. She is also noted for her Mudhead Kachinas, miniature Mudhead dancers, and Storytellers, one of which is in the Smithsonian collection.

Alma was born in Jemez Pueblo on October 9, 1941, the daughter of a Jemez Indian, Louis Loretto, and a Laguna native, Carrie Reid. Alma notes: "I started pottery at age nine, making salt and pepper shakers. All of my five sisters are potters and also make Nativities." In 1962 she married Delfino Concha and in 1969 they moved to Taos. She has trained each of her seven children in the clay craft, and her daughter Renee was winning awards at age fourteen. Alma teaches catechism to the children of Our Lady of Guadalupe parish in Taos and is proud that a Mother Superior in Rome has one of her Nacimientos and sent her a blessing from Pope Paul.

Figuren, deren Höhe 0,6 bis 4,4 cm beträgt. Aber neuerdings hat sie einige Miniaturgruppen im Stil ihrer größeren Gruppen aus rotem und gelbbraunem Ton gestaltet. Sie ist auch bekannt wegen ihrer Mudhead-Kachinas, Miniatur-Mudhead-Tänzer und Erzählerfiguren, von denen eine in der Dauerausstellung der Smithsonian Institution steht.

Alma wurde als Tochter von Louis Loretto, einem Indianer aus Jemez, und Carrie Reid, die aus Laguna Pueblo stammt, am 9. Oktober 1941 im Jemez Pueblo geboren. Sie bemerkt: "Schon mit neun Jahren begann ich zu töpfern und machte Salz- und Pfefferstreuer. Meine fünf Schwestern sind alle Töpferinnen und machen auch Weihnachtskrippen." Im Jahre 1962 heiratete sie Delfino Concha, und 1969 zogen sie nach Taos um. Sie hat jedes ihrer sieben Kinder in der Töpferkunst ausgebildet, und ihre Tochter Renee erwarb schon mit vierzehn Jahren Auszeichnungen. Alma bringt den Kindern der Gemeinde Unserer Lieben Frau von Guadalupe in Taos den Katechismus bei und ist stolz darauf, daß eine Oberin in Rom eine ihrer Krippen besitzt und ihr den Segen des Papstes Paul geschickt hat.

suaves, pero recientemente ha hecho unos en rojo y color piel, como sus piezas más grandes. Alma también es reconocida por sus "Mudhead" Kachinas, "Mudhead" danzantes en miniatura, y Narradores de Cuentos, uno de los cuales está en la colección del Museo Smithsonian.

Alma nació en el pueblo Jemez, el 9 de octubre de 1941. Es hija de un Indio Jemez, Louis Loretto, y de Carrie Reid, natural de Laguna. Alma señala: "A los nueve años comencé cerámica, haciendo saleros y pimenteros. Mis cinco hermanas son ceramistas y también hacen Nacimientos." En 1962, se casó con Delfino Concha y en 1969 se mudaron a Taos. Les ha enseñado a cada uno de sus siete hijos la artesanía de la arcilla y su hija Renee estaba ganando premios a los catorce años. Alma da clases de catecismo a los niños de la parroquia de Nuestra Señora de Guadalupe en Taos y se siente orgullosa de que una Madre Superiora en Roma tenga uno de sus Nacimientos y de que le enviara la bendición del Papa Pablo.

ADDITIONAL NATIVITY ARTISANS

Included here are twenty artists representing eleven pueblos and tribes. Four New Mexico pueblos not represented in the main text are added — Isleta, Nambé, San Felipe, and Santo Domingo. The artisans' production of Nativity scenes is variable: some work at the craft year-round; others only do an occasional set or sets around Christmas. Several of the artists just started making Nativities within the past year, and undoubtedly there will be others entering the field in the coming year.

ACOMA PUEBLO

LILLIAN SALVADOR is ranked as a "Master Potter" of Acoma and uses the traditional Acoma clays and colors. Though a set she made in 1977 is believed to have been her first, it is very finely modeled and detailed. It included thirteen pieces with figures ranging to three inches in height; the Three Wise Men wear pointed hats, a feature only occasionally found in pueblo sets.

FRANCES TORIVIO began making Nativities several years ago. The figures range from 1½ to 4 inches high and are realistically modeled with clearly defined arms and legs and extensive detailing. She uses the typical white Acoma clay with details in orange and black. She lives in the Acoma village of McCarty's.

COCHITI PUEBLO

LOUIS and VIRGINIA NARANJO are a husband-and-wife team who share all phases in producing their Nativities — modeling, sanding, painting, and firing. When they began about

ZUSÄTZLICHE KRIPPENBILDNER

In diesem Kapitel werden zwanzig Künstler aufgeführt, die elf Pueblos und Stämme vertreten. Vier Pueblos von New Mexico, die im Hauptteil des Textes nicht vertreten sind, werden hinzugefügt: Isleta, Nambé, San Felipe und Santo Domingo. Die Krippenproduktion dieser Künstler ist unterschiedlich; manche arbeiten das ganze Jahr hindurch auf diesem Gebiet; andere machen nur gelegentlich zur Weihnachtszeit eine oder mehrere Krippen. Manche haben erst während des letzten Jahres angefangen, Weihnachtskrippen zu gestalten, und zweifellos werden im kommenden Jahr auch andere auf diesem Gebiet zu arbeiten beginnen.

ACOMA PUEBLO

LILLIAN SALVADOR gilt als eine "Meistertöpferin" Acomas und gebraucht die traditionellen Acoma Tone und Farben. Obwohl eine 1977 von ihr angefertigte Gruppe für ihre erste Krippe gehalten wird, ist sie sehr fein modelliert und detailliert. Sie enthält dreizehn Figuren, welche bis 7,6 cm hoch sind; die drei Weisen tragen spitze Hüte, eine Besonderheit, die man nur gelegentlich in Pueblo-Gruppen findet.

FRANCES TORIVIO hat vor mehreren Jahren angefangen, Weihnachtskrippen zu gestalten. Die Figuren variieren von 3,8 bis 10,2 cm Höhe und sind wirklichkeitsnah modelliert, mit deutlich gestalteten Armen und Beinen und vielen Details. Sie gebraucht den typischen weißen Ton Acomas mit orangefarbigen und schwarzen Details. Sie wohnt in dem Acoma-Dorf McCarty's.

COCHITI PUEBLO

LOUIS und VIRGINIA NARANJO sind ein Ehepartner-Team und teilen alle Etappen ihrer Weihnachtskrippenproduktion — das Modellieren, Abschmirgeln, Bemalen und Brennen — miteinander. Als sie vor etwa acht

ARTESANOS ADICIONALES DE NACIMIENTOS

Incluidos aquí hay veinte artistas que representan once pueblos y tribus. Cuatro pueblos de Nuevo México que no aparecen en el texto principal se agregan: Isleta, Nambé, San Felipe, y Santo Domingo. La creación de Nacimientos de estos artesanos varía: algunos trabajan con el artesanía todo el año, otros solo hacen uno que otro juego para Navidad. Varios de los artistas acaban de hacer Nacimientos el año pasado, y sin duda habrá otros que participarán el año que viene.

EL PUEBLO ACOMA

LILLIAN SALVADOR está clasificada como una "Ceramista Magistral" de Acoma; usa los colores y la arcilla tradicional de ese pueblo. Aunque se cree que en 1977 hizo su primer juego, éste está muy finamente modelado y detallado. Incluyó trece piezas con figuras de hasta 7.6 centímetros de alto. Los Tres Reyes Magos llevan sombreros de copa alta, una característica que sólo se encuentra ocasionalmente en las colecciones de los pueblos.

FRANCES TORIVIO comenzó a hacer Nacimientos hace algunos años. Las figuras miden de 3.8 a 10.2 centímetros de alto y están modeladas en forma realista, con brazos y piernas bien definidos y con muchos detalles. Emplea la típica arcilla blanca de Acoma con detalles en naranja y negro. Vive en la aldea Acoma de McCarty's.

EL PUEBLO COCHITI

Los esposos LOUIS y VIRGINIA NARANJO comparten todas las fases en la creación se sus Nacimientos — modelado, lijado, pintado, y cocido al fuego. Cuando comenzaron hace ocho

UNKNOWN PAPAGO CHILD
  1-piece set   ½–2″ high   ca. 1975
This was found at a Franciscan fair of Papago
children's art. It is all in one piece with the
seven figures and a ramada modeled of clay on
a clay disk which is 7½ inches in diameter.
The figures range from ½ inch for the
Baby Jesus in his crib to 1⅛ inches high for
the adults and animal. The Holy Family is
thoughtfully placed under the ramada, a
popular structure among the Papago living in
the hot desert country of Arizona. Approaching
with proper reverence are the Three Wise Men.
Mr. and Mrs. Bruce Irwin, Phoenix, Arizona.

UNBEKANNTES PAPAGO KIND
  Gruppe aus einem Stück
  1.25 bis 5 cm hoch   ca. 1975
Diese Gruppe wurde in einer von den
Franziskanern organisierten Ausstellung von
Kunstwerken Jugendlicher entdeckt. Die sieben
Figuren und die *Ramada* sind aus einem
Stück Ton gemacht und stehen auf einer
runden Tonscheibe mit einem Durchmesser von
18.7 cm. Die Höhe der Figuren variiert von
1.25 cm für das Jesuskind in der Krippe bis zu
2.8 cm für die Erwachsenen und die Tiere.
Die Heilige Familie ist rücksichtsvoll unter die
Ramada gestellt, ein Schattendach auf
Pfosten, das bei den Papago-Indianern im
heißen Wüstengebiet Arizonas sehr beliebt ist.
Die drei Weisen nähern sich mit gebührender
Ehrfurcht. Herr und Frau Bruce Irwin,
Phoenix, Arizona.

NIÑO PAPAGO DESCONOCIDO   juego de
  1 pieza   de 1.37 cm. a 5 cm. de alto
  circa 1975
Esta pieza se encontró en una Feria Fran-
ciscana de Arte de Niños Pápagos. Consiste
de una sola pieza con las siete figuras y una
ramada modelada en arcilla en un disco de
17.5 centímetros de diámetro. Las figuras miden
de 1.25 centímetros de alto, como el Niño Jesús
en su cuna, a 3 centímetros de alto por los
adultos y el animal. Con mucha previsión la
Sagrada Familia está colocada bajo la ramada,
una estructura muy popular entre los Indios
Pápago que habitan en el desierto cálido de
Arizona. Los Tres Reyes Magos se acercan con
toda reverencia. Señor y señora Bruce Irwin,
Phoenix, Arizona.

eight years ago, they included Wise Men and shepherds in their sets, but now they are doing eight- to nine-piece sets with just the Holy Family and animals. Instead of the usual domestic animals, they are including wild animals such as deer, bears, foxes, and antelopes. Louis is the son of Frances Naranjo Suina.

SERAFINA ORTIZ uses a white slip with considerable detailing in orange and black. Her style is rustic in feeling and incorporates several unique details, such as in an eleven-piece set made in 1976: several figures are attached to pedestals, fingernails are delineated, and the Wise Men have beards painted on; the crib is a cradleboard set on four legs, resembling the cross-legged wood style but made entirely of clay; a camel is included among the animals. The size range is 2¼ to 4 inches high.

AURELIA SUINA is the mother-in-law of Ada Suina. Though she has long been noted for her pots and figurative work, she began making Nativities just recently. Her work is sought after by experienced collectors because she works in the old way, using only native materials and traditional techniques, such as polishing the slips, which gives her pieces a fine patina.

ISLETA PUEBLO

STELLA TELLER does figures of polished whiteware with detailing in red and black. Her nine-piece sets have figures ranging from 3 to 3½ inches high and include an angel and five animals, with two unusual additions to the customary ox and donkey — a mountain sheep or "bighorn," and two pigs. She sometimes makes stables in the ramada style, fashioned entirely of unbaked clay, including the upright posts and ceiling beams.

Jahren anfingen, haben sie ihren Gruppen Weise und Hirten beigegeben, aber jetzt bestehen ihre Gruppen von acht bis neun Figuren ausschließlich aus der Heiligen Familie und den Tieren. Anstatt der gewöhnlichen Haustiere geben sie ihren Figuren wilde Tiere — zum Beispiel Hirsche, Bären, Füchse und Antilopen — bei. Louis ist der Sohn von Frances Naranjo Suina.

SERAFINA ORTIZ benutzt einen weißen geschlämmten Überzug mit viel Detaillierung in Orange und Schwarz. Ihr Stil hat einen ländlichen Charakter und schließt mehrere Besonderheiten ein: beispielsweise in einer 1976 angefertigten Gruppe von elf Figuren sind mehrere Figuren auf Sockeln befestigt, Fingernägel sind genau ausgeführt, und die Weisen tragen angemalte Bärte; die Krippe ist eine auf vier Beinen ruhende Indianerkrippe (cradleboard), die dem Holzstil mit gekreuzten Beinen ähnelt, aber ganz aus Ton gestaltet ist; ein Kamel ist den anderen Tieren beigegeben. Die Größe der Figuren variiert von 5,7 bis 10,2 cm Höhe.

AURELIA SUINA ist die Schwiegermutter Ada Suinas. Obwohl sie schon seit langem wegen ihrer Töpfe und figürlichen Arbeiten bekannt ist, hat sie erst vor kurzem angefangen, Weihnachtskrippen zu gestalten. Ihre Schöpfungen werden von sachkundigen Sammlern gesucht, weil sie nur auf die alte Weise arbeitet, indem sie nur örtlich vorkommende Materialien und herkömmliche Methoden anwendet; sie poliert zum Beispiel die geschlämmten Überzüge, was ihren Gestalten eine glänzende Patina verleiht.

ISLETA PUEBLO

STELLA TELLER gestaltet Figuren aus poliertem weißem Ton mit Detaillierung in Rot und Schwarz. Die Gestalten ihrer Neunfigurengruppen sind von 7,6 bis 8,9 cm hoch und schließen einen Engel und fünf Tiere ein; zwei ungewöhnliche Tiere — ein Dickhornschaf ("bighorn") und zwei Schweine — werden dem üblichen Ochs und Esel hinzugefügt. Manchmal fertigt sie Ställe im Ramada-Stil an, die völlig aus ungebranntem Ton gestaltet werden, einschließlich der Pfosten und Balken.

años, incluían en sus juegos Reyes Magos y pastores, pero sus juegos ahora son de ocho a nueve piezas con la Sagrada Familia y animales solamente. En lugar de los animales domésticos corrientes, incluyen animales salvajes como por ejemplo venados, osos, zorros, y antílopes. Louis es hijo de Frances Naranjo Suina.

SERAFINA ORTIZ emplea un sellador blanco con considerable detalles en naranja y negro. Su estilo es de sentimiento rústico e incorpora varios detalles únicos; por ejemplo, en un juego de once piezas que hizo en 1976, varias figuras están unidas a pedestales, las uñas están delineadas, y los Reyes Magos tienen barbas pintadas; la cuna es una cuna portátil, descansa sobre cuatro patas, parecida a la del estilo de patas de madera cruzadas pero hecha totalmente de arcilla; entre los animales hay incluido un camello. El tamaño de estas figuras varía de 5.7 a 10.2 centímetros de alto.

AURELIA SUINA es la suegra de Ada Suina. Aunque hace tiempo se la ha conocido por sus ollas y obras figurativas, empezó a hacer Nacimientos recientemente. Los expertos coleccionistas se interesan por su obra porque emplea métodos antiguos, usando sólamente materiales nativos y técnicas tradicionales, como por ejemplo puliendo los selladores lo cual le da a sus piezas una pátina fina.

EL PUEBLO ISLETA

STELLA TELLER hace figuras de arcilla blanca pulida con detalles en rojo y negro. Sus juegos de nueve piezas contienen figuras que miden de 7.6 a 8.9 centímetros de alto e incluyen un ángel, cinco animales y, además del buey y el burro corriente, otros dos que raramente aparecen: una oveja de montaña (oveja grande de las Montañas Rocosas) y dos puercos. A veces hace establos al estilo "ramada," creados completamente de arcilla sin cocer, incluyendo los postes derechos y las vigas del techo.

JEMEZ PUEBLO

MARY TOYA is the sister of Alma Concha and Dorothy Trujillo. Her figures are 1½ to 5¾ inches high and are characterized by large heads set on rounded bodies in a kneeling position with just the feet visible. They are made of the buff-colored Jemez clay and wrapped in intricately patterned blankets of terra cotta and black.

FANNY WALL is another sister of Alma Concha and Dorothy Trujillo. After formal art training, she recently returned to her native Jemez and has done large figures of the Madonna and Child and Holy Family, as well as Nativity scenes. These are usually seven to eight pieces with very small figures, almost miniatures, in Jemez Clay.

NAMBE PUEBLO

MARIE HERRERA does different styles but is perhaps best known for her micaceous clay figures, on which she uses a minimum of detailing, just a touch to delineate eyes and mouths. The figures are large and rather primitive, but the faces have great character and, as one expert notes: "They have a very definite folk art feeling."

PAPAGO

THOMAS FRANCO is the son of Chepa and the late Domingo Franco and works in their unique style and materials. He carves his figures of saguaro cactus rib; they are large — some as high as six inches for animals and fourteen inches for humans. He also makes stables in the ramada style with pinewood floors and small mesquite branches for the posts and beams. His wife makes the clothes, accessories, and hair pieces for the figures.

JEMEZ PUEBLO

MARY TOYA ist die Schwester von Alma Concha und Dorothy Trujillo. Ihre Figuren sind 3,8 bis 14,6 cm hoch und haben charakteristisch große Köpfe auf rundlichen Körpern; sie knieen, so daß nur die Füße sichtbar sind. Sie werden aus dem braungelben Jemez Ton modelliert und in kompliziert gemusterte Decken aus Terrakotta und Schwarz eingewickelt.

FANNY WALL ist eine weitere Schwester Alma Conchas und Dorothy Trujillos. Nach künstlerischer Fachausbildung kehrte sie vor kurzem in ihr Heimat-Pueblo Jemez zurück, wo sie sowohl große Figuren der Madonna mit dem Kinde und der Heiligen Familie, als auch Weihnachtskrippen gestaltet hat. Gewöhnlich bestehen diese aus sieben bis acht sehr kleinen Gestalten, fast Miniaturen, aus Jemez Ton.

NAMBE PUEBLO

MARIE HERRERA arbeitet in verschiedenen Stilrichtungen, ist aber vielleicht wegen ihrer Figuren aus glimmerhaltigem Ton am besten bekannt, die sie mit einem Minimum an Details bemalt — gerade genug, um Augen und Mund anzudeuten. Die Gestalten sind groß und ziemlich primitiv, aber die Gesichter zeigen ausdrucksvolle Charakterzüge und, wie ein Fachmann bemerkt: "Ihnen wohnt ein besonderes Gefühl der Volkskunst inne."

PAPAGO

THOMAS FRANCO, der Sohn Chepas und des verstorbenen Domingo Franco, arbeitet im einzigartigen Stil seiner Eltern und mit denselben Materialien. Er schnitzt seine Figuren aus Saguaro-Kaktusrippen; sie sind groß — manche Tiere bis 15,2 cm und manche Menschen bis 35,6 cm. Er gestaltet auch Ställe im Ramada-Stil mit Kiefernholzböden und kleinen Mesquite-Ästen als Pfähle und Balken. Seine Frau fertigt Kleider, Zubehör und Haartrachten für die Figuren an.

EL PUEBLO JEMEZ

MARY TOYA es hermana de Alma Concha y Dorothy Trujillo. Sus figuras miden 3.8 a 14.6 centímetros de alto y se caracterizan por poseer cabezas grandes sobre cuerpos redondeados, arrodillados que sólo dejan ver los pies. Están hechos con la arcilla de color piel de Jemez y cubiertos con mantas de diseños complicados de color terra cota y negro.

FANNY WALL es otra de las hermanas de Alma Concha y Dorothy Trujillo. Después de un entrenamiento artístico académico, volvió hace poco a su Jemez natal y ha hecho figuras grandes de la Virgen y el Niño y la Sagrada Familia así como también Nacimientos. Estos contienen generalmente siete u ocho piezas con figuras muy pequeñas, casi en miniatura, de arcilla de Jemez.

EL PUEBLO NAMBE

MARIE HERRERA emplea estilos diferentes pero tal vez sea más conocida por sus figuras de arcilla micácea con un mínimo de detalles, simplemente un toque para delinear los ojos y las bocas. Sus figuras son grandes, más bien primitivas, pero los rostros poseen carácter, y como lo señala un experto: "Poseen un sentimiento artístico y folklórico muy definidos."

PAPAGO

THOMAS FRANCO es hijo de Chepa y el fallecido Domingo Franco; trabaja con el estilo y materiales exclusivos de ellos. Crea sus figuras del nervios del cactos saguaro; son grandes — algunos de los animales miden hasta 15.2 centímetros de alto y algunas figuras humanas hasta 35.6 centímetros. También hace establos de estilo "ramada" con pisos de madera de pino y, para los postes y vigas, emplea ramas de mezquite. Su esposa hace la ropa, los adornos, y las pelucas para las figuras.

SAN FELIPE PUEBLO

LUPE LUCERO is another sister of Alma Concha and Dorothy Trujillo, one of the six Loretto sisters from Jemez. She started making Nativities in 1978. They are similar to Alma's in color but are more traditional and have more detailing. Characteristic of her faces are the round mouth and little eyes.

SAN ILDEFONSO PUEBLO

YELLOWBIRD is the Indian name of Jose V. Aguilar, brother of Alfred Aguilar. In 1975 he started doing miniatures in polished blackware but is now doing larger figures, around five inches high, in nine-piece sets. One of his large blackware sets took Third Prize at the 1978 New Mexico State Fair. In it the Wise Men carried bows and arrows and wore real turquoise necklaces and cloth headbands with a feather.

SANTA CLARA PUEBLO

NICK and LINDA HALSEY began doing miniatures in 1978. The figures, ranging from ⅝ to 1½ inches high, are done in blackware with polished and unpolished areas and have the look of contemporary sculpture. Their nine-piece sets include the Holy Family, Three Wise Men, and three animals, plus three tiny gifts. The Wise Men are interpreted in eagle, owl, and human shapes and are designed to hold the tiny gifts in their laps. The Baby Jesus, also separate, fits into the lap of the Virgin.

MARTHA MIRABAL is the daughter of Maria I. Naranjo and is noted for her miniature sets. They range from ½ to 1½ inches high and are done in either red, black, white, or natural buff-colored clay with polished surfaces. She also does various types of animals that may be added to the sets.

SAN FELIPE PUEBLO

LUPE LUCERO ist eine andere Schwester Alma Conchas und Dorothy Trujillos, eine der sechs Loretto Schwestern aus Jemez. 1978 begann sie, Weihnachtskrippen zu gestalten. In den Farben gleichen sie denjenigen Almas, aber sie sind traditioneller und haben mehr Details. Ein Merkmal ihrer Gesichter ist der runde Mund und die kleinen Augen.

SAN ILDEFONSO PUEBLO

YELLOWBIRD ist der indianische Name José V. Aguilars; er ist der Bruder von Alfred Aguilar. 1975 fing er an, Miniaturen aus poliertem schwarzem Ton zu gestalten, aber jetzt macht er größere, circa 13 cm hohe Gestalten in Gruppen von neun Figuren. Eine seiner großen Schwarztongruppen hat bei der Staatsausstellung von New Mexico den dritten Preis erworben. In dieser Gruppe trugen die Weisen Pfeile und Bögen, gediegene Türkishalsketten und tuchene Kopfbänder mit einer Feder.

SANTA CLARA PUEBLO

NICK und LINDA HALSEY fingen im Jahre 1978 an, Miniaturen zu gestalten. Die von 1,6 bis 3,8 cm hohen Figuren werden in schwarzem Ton mit polierten und unpolierten Flächen ausgeführt und sehen wie zeitgenössische Plastiken aus. Ihre Neunfigurengruppen enthalten die Heilige Familie, die drei Weisen, drei Tiere und drei winzige Geschenke. Die Weisen sind in Adler-, Eulen- und Menschengestalt dargestellt, und werden so geformt, daß sie die winzigen Geschenke im Schoß halten. Das Christkind, auch eine Einzelfigur, paßt in den Schoß der Heiligen Jungfrau.

MARTHA MIRABAL ist die Tochter von Maria I. Naranjo und ist wegen ihrer Miniaturgruppen bekannt. Sie variieren von 1,3 bis 3,8 cm Höhe und werden entweder in rotem, schwarzem, weißem oder natürlichem braungelbem Ton mit polierten Flächen ausgeführt. Sie fertigt auch verschiedene Tierarten an, die den Gruppen beigegeben werden können.

EL PUEBLO SAN FELIPE

LUPE LUCERO es otra de las hermanas de Alma Concha y Dorothy Trujillo, una de las seis hermanas Loretto de Jemez. Comenzó a hacer Nacimientos en 1978. Son semejantes a los de Alma en color, aunque son más tradicionales y contienen más detalles. Los rostros de sus figuras se caracterizan por las bocas redondeadas y los ojos pequeños.

EL PUEBLO SAN ILDEFONSO

YELLOWBIRD es el nombre indio de José V. Aguilar, hermano de Alfred Aguilar. En 1975 comenzó a hacer figuras en miniatura de arcilla negra pulida; ahora hace figuras más grandes, aproximadamente de 13 centímetros de alto, en juegos de nueve piezas. Uno de sus juegos grandes de arcilla negra recibió el Tercer Premio en la Feria del Estado de Nuevo México en 1978. En ese juego, los Reyes Magos llevaban arcos y flechas y vestían cintas de cabello de tela con plumas y collares de turquesas verdaderas.

EL PUEBLO SANTA CLARA

NICK y LINDA HALSEY comenzaron a hacer figuras en miniatura en 1978. Estas figuras, de casi 1.6 a 3.8 centímetros de alto, están hechas en arcilla negra con partes pulidas y partes sin pulir y poseen la apariencia de esculturas contemporáneas. Los juegos de nueve piezas de estos artistas contienen la Sagrada Familia, los Tres Reyes Magos, y tres animales, además de tres pequeños regalos. Los Reyes Magos aparecen en forma de águila, lechuza, y humana y están diseñados de tal forma que pueden sostener los pequeñísimos regalos en sus regazos. El Niño Jesús, también separado, cabe en el regazo de la Virgen.

MARTHA MIRABAL es hija de María I. Naranjo y es conocida por sus juegos en miniatura. Miden 1.3 a 3.8 centímetros de alto y están hechos de arcilla de color rojo, o negro, o blanco, o piel natural, de superficies pulidas. También hace varios tipos de animales que se pueden agregar al juego.

MADELINE NARANJO is a prize-winning potter who began making Nacimientos in 1972. She does blackware figures with all-polished surfaces, ranging from three to six inches high. In one of her seven-piece sets with the larger size figures, Mary and Joseph have cupped hands creating an opening so they can hold flowers or small candles. Her clay cradles have a distinctive shield shape.

BETSY REVAL is a former resident of Santa Clara who now lives on the Navajo reservation. A fifteen-piece set that she did in 1972 is of polished blackware with matte areas on the faces. The figures range from 1 inch for the smallest animal to 4½ inches for the people. Unique features are the deep box-shaped cradle and the elegantly draped clothes fashioned in an Oriental style.

CLARA STONE won the Best of Contemporary award at a juried show in Denver in 1978, though she only began doing Nativity scenes recently. The prize-winning five-piece set was done in unpolished blackware in a dramatic contemporary style. The largest figure was three inches high with a feather headdress modeled in clay.

SANTO DOMINGO PUEBLO

EDNA CORIZ is another of the six Loretto sisters born in Jemez (Alma Concha and Dorothy Trujillo, etc.). She made her first Nativity in 1976. Her style is similar to her sister Mary Toya's, but she works in Santo Domingo's red clay, using a white slip with detailing in black.

MADELINE NARANJO ist eine Töpferin, die viele Preise erworben hat, und die seit 1972 Nacimientos produziert. Sie macht Schwarzton-figuren mit ganz polierten Flächen, die von 7,6 bis 15,2 cm hoch sind. In einer ihrer Gruppen von sieben größeren Figuren haben Maria und Joseph die Hände so gewölbt, daß eine Öffnung für Blumen oder kleine Kerzen entsteht. Ihre Krippen aus Ton haben die einmalige Form eines Schildes.

BETSY REVAL ist eine ehemalige Einwohnerin Santa Claras, die jetzt im Navajo-Reservat lebt. Eine Gruppe von fünfzehn Figuren, die sie 1972 angefertigt hat, ist aus poliertem Schwarzton mit matten Stellen in den Gesich-tern. Die Gestalten variieren von 2,5 cm für das kleinste Tier bis 11,4 cm für die Menschen. Einzigartige Merkmale sind die tiefe, büchsen-förmige Wiege und die elegant drapierten Kleider, die in orientalischem Stil angefertigt sind.

CLARA STONE gewann 1978 den ersten Preis für zeitgenössische Kunst an einer Ausstellung in Denver obwohl sie erst vor kurzem angefangen hat, Weihnachtskrippen zu gestal-ten. Die preisgekrönte Gruppe von fünf Figuren wurde aus unpoliertem Schwarzton in einem dramatischen zeitgenössischen Stil ausgeführt. Die größte Figur war 7,6 cm hoch mit einem aus Ton modellierten Federkopfschmuck.

SANTO DOMINGO PUEBLO

EDNA CORIZ ist eine weitere der in Jemez geborenen Loretto Schwestern. Im Jahre 1976 gestaltete sie ihre erste Weihnachtskrippe. Ihr Stil ähnelt dem ihrer Schwester Mary Toya, aber sie arbeitet mit dem roten Ton von Santo Domingo, wobei sie einen weißen geschlämmten Überzug mit schwarzer Detaillierung verwendet.

MADELINE NARANJO es una ceramista que ha ganado premios y que comenzó a hacer Nacimientos en 1972. Hace figuras de arcilla negra con todas las superficies pulidas; miden de 7.6 a 15.2 centímetros de alto. En uno de sus juegos de siete piezas con figuras de tamaño más grande, María y José tienen las manos juntas formando una cavidad para sostener flores o pequeñas velas. Sus cunas de arcilla poseen la forma distintiva de un escudo.

BETSY REVAL es una antigua residente de Santa Clara y ahora vive en la Reservación Navajo. Un juego de quince piezas que hizo en 1972 está hecho de arcilla negra pulida con partes en los rostros en tono mate. Las figuras miden de 2.5 centímetros de alta para el animal más pequeño a 11.4 centímetros de alto para las personas. Algunas de las características exclusivas son la cuna honda en forma de caja y ropas que caen elegantemente, hechas al estilo oriental.

CLARA STONE recibió el Premio Contempo-ráneo que un jurado le otorgó en una exposición en Denver, en 1978, aunque sólo hace poco tiempo que comenzó a hacer Nacimientos. El juego que fue premiado contiene cinco piezas y está hecho en arcilla negra sin pulir en un fuerte estilo contemporáneo. La figura mayor mide 7.6 centímetros de alto, con un adorno de plumas en la cabeza hecho de arcilla.

EL PUEBLO SANTO DOMINGO

EDNA CORIZ es otra de las seis hermanas Loretto, nacida en Jemez (Alma Concha y Dorothy Trujillo, etc.). Hizo su primer Naci-miento en 1976. Su estilo se asemeja al de su hermana Mary Toya, pero trabaja con la arcilla roja de Santo Domingo y emplea un sellador de color blanco con detalles en negro.

TESUQUE PUEBLO

ANNA MARIE LOVATO, the daughter of Manuel Vigil, has not made Nativity scenes for many years, but should be mentioned here because she was second only to her father as the earliest Nativity artisan. She did the painted Colonial style in eleven- to fourteen-piece sets that were beautifully detailed in pastels and bright colors with gilt accents. One of these sets was in the Alexander Girard Nativities exhibit at the Museum of International Folk Art in 1961.

ADAM TRUJILLO's figures reflect the characteristics of the Tesuque Rain Gods as represented in the twentieth century. His human figures are set on clay pedestals and painted in bright poster colors after firing, typical of current Tesuque techniques. His sets have an average of fourteen figures ranging to a height of five inches. One of his sets took First Prize in 1977 at a juried show in Denver.

TESUQUE PUEBLO

ANNA MARIE LOVATO, die Tochter Manuel Vigils, hat seit vielen Jahren keine Weihnachtskrippen mehr gestaltet, soll aber hier erwähnt werden, weil sie nach ihrem Vater die zweite Person war, die Weihnachtskrippen anfertigte. Sie machte im bemalten Kolonialstil Gruppen von elf bis vierzehn Figuren, die in Pastell- und hellen Farben mit goldfarbenen Akzenten sehr schön detailliert wurden. Eine dieser Gruppen befand sich 1961 in der Alexander Girard-Weihnachtskrippenausstellung im Museum für Internationale Volkskunst.

ADAM TRUJILLOs Gestalten spiegeln die besonderen Merkmale der im 20. Jahrhundert dargestellten Tesuque Regengötter wider. Seine Menschengestalten werden nach dem Brennen auf Tonsockel gestellt und mit hellen Plakatfarben bemalt, ein typisches Arbeitsverfahren im heutigen Tesuque. Seine Gruppen enthalten durchschnittlich vierzehn Figuren, die eine Höhe von 12,7 cm erreichen. Eine seiner Gruppen hat 1977 den ersten Preis in einer Kunstausstellung in Denver erhalten.

EL PUEBLO TESUQUE

ANNA MARIE LOVATO, hija de Manuel Vigil, no ha hecho Nacimientos por muchos años, pero debemos mencionarla aquí porque fue la segunda, después de su padre, entre los primeros artesanos de Nacimientos. Empleó el estilo Colonial pintado, en juegos de 11 a 14 piezas hermosamente detallados en colores suaves y brillantes con acentos dorados. Uno de estos juegos se exhibió en la exposición Alexander Girard de Nacimientos en el Museo de Arte Folklórico Internacional en 1961.

Las figuras de ADAM TRUJILLO reflejan las características de los Dioses de la Lluvia de Tesuque en una interpretación del siglo XX. Sus figuras humanas están colocadas sobre los pedestales de arcilla y, después de cocerlas al fuego, pintadas en colores de carteles brillantes, típico de las técnicas actuales de Tesuque. Sus juegos poseen un promedio de 14 figuras que miden hasta 12.7 centímetros de alto. En 1977 el jurado de una exposición en Denver le otorgó el Primer Premio a uno de sus juegos.

NOTES TO THE INTRODUCTION   ANMERKUNGEN ZUR EINLEITUNG   ANOTACIONES DE LA INTRODUCCIÓN

1. Lange 1975, p. 89
2. Sullivan 1977, p. 116
3. Raggio 1969
4. *Denver Post* 13 December 1964
5. Houtzager 1973
6. Houtzager 1979, personal correspondence: International Association of Friends of the Crib, with headquarters in Rome:
   Associazione Italiana Amici del Presepio
   Via Tor de' Conti 31/A
   Roma 00184
   Attention: Signore Angelo Stefanucci
7. Frank and Harlow 1974, p. 8
8. Dickey 1949, 1970, p. 234
9. Boyd 1969, pp. 3–24
10. Frank 1976, p. 8
11. Boyd 1969, p. 23
12. Toulouse 1976, pp. 19, 27, 28
13. Among them: Celso Gallegos, José Dolores López, José Mondragón, George López, Gloria López Córdova, Nicodemus López

bibliography   literatur-verzeichnis   bibliografía

Boyd, E. "The New Mexico Santero." *El Palacio*, Spring 1969.

_____. *Popular Arts of Spanish New Mexico*. Santa Fe: Museum of New Mexico Press, 1974.

Breese, Frances, and Boyd, E. *New Mexico Santos: How to Name Them*. Santa Fe: Museum of New Mexico International Folk Art Foundation, 1966.

Denver Post, Sunday Empire Magazine. "Once Upon a Christmas." An article on the December 1964 display of Nativities and other Christmas art at the Denver Art Museum. 13 December 1964.

Dickey, Roland F. *New Mexico Village Arts*. 1949. Reprint. Albuquerque: University of New Mexico Press, 1970.

Dominguez, Fray Francisco Atanasio. *The Missions of New Mexico, 1776: A Description by Fray Francisco Atanasio Dominguez With Other Contemporary Documents*. 1956. Translated and Annotated by Eleanor B. Adams and Fray Angelico Chavez. Reprint. Albuquerque: University of New Mexico Press, 1975.

Ferguson, George. *Signs and Symbols In Christian Art*. New York: Oxford University Press, 1954.

Ferrandis, Pilar. *Nacimientos: Exposición En El Museo Nacional De Artes Decorativas*. Artes Decorativas En España, vol. 4. Madrid: A Frodisio Aquado, S.A., 1950.

Foley, Daniel J. *Little Saints of Christmas: The Santons of Provence*. Boston: Dresser, Chapman, & Grimes, Inc , 1959.

Frank, Larry. *The Taos News*, 16 September 1976.

Frank, Larry, and Harlow, Francis. *Historic Pottery of the Pueblo Indians: 1600–1880*. Boston: New York Graphic Society, 1974.

Girard, Alexander. *The Nativity: The Church Festival Commemorating the Birth of Jesus*. A catalog of the exhibition of the Girard Foundation collection of Nativities at the Museum of International Folk Art in 1961. Santa Fe: Museum of International Folk Art, 1961.

Gratz, Kathleen. "Origins of the Tesuque Rain God." *El Palacio*, Fall 1976.

Hallmark Cards. *The Nativity 1963*. An engagement calendar featuring twelve reproductions from the Girard collection of Nativities in an exhibition in Kansas City, Missouri in 1962–1963 with notes by J. Hall and Alexander Girard. Kansas City: Hallmark Cards, 1962.

Hanley, Frank L., and Gueno, Jeffery G. "The Historical Creche." *Hobbies — The Magazine For Collectors*, December 1976.

Houtzager, Maria Elisabeth. *Kerstkribben In De Volkskunst*. A catalog of an exhibition of Dr. Houtzager's international collection of Nativities and folk art held at Philips Ontspannings Centrium, Eindhoven, Netherlands, December 21, 1973 to January 20, 1974.

Lange, Yvonne. "Santos: The Household Wooden Saints of Puerto Rico." Ph.D. dissertation, University of Pennsylvania, 1975.

_____. "El Nacimiento: The Christmas Crib." Xeroxed. Santa Fe: Museum of International Folk Art, 19 December 1975.

Maxwell Museum of Anthropology. *Seven Families in Pueblo Pottery.* Albuquerque: University of New Mexico, 1974.

Monthan, Guy and Doris. *Art and Indian Individualists: The Art of Seventeen Contemporary Southwestern Artists and Craftsmen.* Flagstaff: Northland Press, 1975.

————. "Helen Cordero." *American Indian Art Magazine,* Autumn 1977.

New Mexico Magazine. "The Nativity in Folk Art." November-December 1962.

Ortiz, Alfonso, ed. *New Perspectives on the Pueblos.* A School of American Research Book. Douglas W. Schwartz, General Editor. Albuquerque: University of New Mexico Press, 1972.

Raggio, Olga. *The Nativity: The Christmas Creche at the Metropolitan Museum of Art.* The Loretta Hines Howard Collection. Garden City, New York: Doubleday & Co., Inc., 1965.

Redfield, Robert. "The Folk Culture of Yucatan." 1941. Reprinted in anthology, *Anthropology of Folk Religion,* edited by Charles Leslie. New York: Random House, Vintage Books, 1960.

Sullivan, Rosemary D. "The Santons of Provence." *Hobbies — The Magazine for Collectors,* December 1977.

————. "Creches: Miniature Mangers." In *The Encyclopedia of Collectibles.* Alexandria, Virginia: Time-Life Books, 1978.

Tanner, Clara Lee. *Southwest Indian Craft Arts.* Tucson: University of Arizona Press, 1968.

Toulouse, Betty. "Pueblo Pottery Traditions: Ever Constant, Ever Changing." *El Palacio,* Fall 1976.

Trimble, Marshall. *Arizona: A Panoramic History of a Frontier State.* New York: Doubleday & Co., Inc., 1977.

Tryk, Sheila. "Artists and the Holy Family." *New Mexico Magazine,* December 1976.

Wilson, Maggie. "The Beauty Makers." Special Edition: "Southwestern Pottery Today." *Arizona Highways,* May 1974.

Winn, Robert K. *Viva Jesus, María, y José: A Celebration of the Birth of Jesus.* Mexican Folk Art and Toys from the Collection of R. K. Winn. San Antonio, Texas: Trinity University Press, 1977.

INDEX   REGISTER   INDICE

OTHER BOOKS FROM AVANYU PUBLISHING

Tonita Peña *by Samuel L. Gray.*
The biography of the remarkably talented first female pueblo artist from Cochiti Pueblo, New Mexico with numerous color examples of her art. Cloth $39.95, Paper $29.95 plus $2.25 shipping.

C.N. Cotton and His Navajo Blankets *by Lester L. Williams, M.D.*
A biography of the premier Navajo trader and blanket dealer accompanied by reprints of his early mail order catalogs. 13 color, 48 black & white plates. Paper $22.50 plus $2.25 shipping.

The Mimbres, Art and Archaeology *by Jesse Walter Fewkes.*
Three essays, originally published between 1914 and 1934, on these unique aborigines from southern New Mexico, with an essay by J.J. Brody. 182 pp., 300 illus. Cloth $29.95, Paper $16.95 plus $2.25 shipping.

A Little History of the Navajos *by Oscar H. Lipps.*
A reprint of an eyewitness' 1909 view of the history of the Navajo Indians. 136 pp., 16 black & white plates. Cloth $19.95 plus $2.00 shipping.

Zuni Fetishism *by Ruth Kirk.*
Originally published in 1948 by *El Palacio, Journal of the Museum of New Mexico,* this study of 25 different pieces collected by the Laboratory of Anthropology brings an expanded understanding to this aspect of Zuni religion and ceremonialism. 72 pp. Paper $4.75 plus $1.25 shipping.

J.B. Moore, U.S. Licensed Indian Trader—A Collection of Catalogs Published at Crystal Trading Post 1903-1911.
Fine Navajo rugs, ceremonial baskets, silverware, jewelry, and curios originally published by Moore. 114 pp., 30 color and black & white plates. Paper $16.50 plus $1.75 shipping.

Pendleton Woolen Mills
A reprint of the 1915 mail order catalog from the world famous Pendleton Woolen Mills of Oregon, featuring photos of patterns, Indians, daily uses, and more. 114 pp., 30 color and black & white plates. Paper $8.50 plus $1.75 shipping.

The Navajo *by J.B. Moore.*
An early mail order Navajo rug catalog, first printed in 1911. 40 pp., 15 color, 18 black & white plates. Paper $12.50 plus $1.50 shipping.

Hopi Snake Ceremonies *by Jesse Walter Fewkes.*
A reprint of two essays dating from 1894 and 1897, describing in detail one of the most famous and spectacular of all Native American ceremonial events. 160 pp., 51 black & white plates. Paper $16.95 plus $1.75 shipping.